THE BEST POLITICAL CARTOONS OF THE YEAR 2007 EDITION

Edited by
Daryl Cagle and
Brian Fairrington

Dedication

This book is dedicated to the millions of loyal fans of our web site at www.cagle.com. We appreciate you!

The Best Political Cartoons of the Year, 2007 Edition

Daryl Cagle, Cartoonist-Editor, Cover
Brian Fairrington, Cartoonist-Editor, Inside Front Cover
Susan Cagle, Writer
Robert A. Bartley, Copy Editor
Laura Norman, Executive Editor for Que Publishing
Thanks to Cagle Cartoons staff: Stacey Fairrington/Cartoon Logistics, Cari Dawson Bartley/Administration, and Brian Davis/Support.

Special thanks to: Tribune Media Services, United Media, Creators Syndicate, Copley News Service and the Washington Post Writers Group.

International Standard Book Number: 0-7897-3655-1
CIP Data Available Upon Request
Printed in the United States of America
First Printing: November 2006

THE BEST POLITICAL CARTOONS OF THE YEAR 2007 EDITION

Table of Contents

About the Editor-Cartoonists

Daryl Cagle

Daryl is the daily editorial cartoonist for MSNBC.com. With more than three million regular, unique users each month, Daryl's editorial cartoon site with Microsoft (www.cagle.com) is the most popular cartoon website of any kind on the Internet. It is also the most widely used education site in social studies classrooms around the world.

For the past 30 years, Daryl has been one of America's most prolific cartoonists. Raised in California, Daryl went to college at UC Santa Barbara and then moved to New York City, where he worked for 10 years with Jim Henson's Muppets, illustrating scores of books, magazines, calendars, and all manner of products. In 2001, Daryl started a new syndicate, Cagle Cartoons, Inc. (www.caglecartoons.com), which distributes the cartoons of 50 editorial cartoonists and columnists to more than 800 newspapers in the United States, Canada, and Latin America. Daryl is a past president of the National Cartoonists Society. He is a frequent guest on Fox News, CNN and MSNBC. Daryl is a popular and entertaining public speaker. Interested in having Daryl speak to your group? Contact us through www.caglecartoons.com for more information.

Brian Fairrington

A graduate of Arizona State University, Brian earned a bachelor's degree in political science and a master's degree in communications.

Brian is one of the most accomplished younger cartoonists in the country. Brian was the recipient of the Locher Award, the Charles M. Schulz Award, and several Society of Professional Journalists awards and Gold Circle Awards. He is a regular on the Phoenix-based television talk show *Horizon*, for which one of his appearances garnered an Emmy award.

Brian's cartoons are nationally syndicated to more than 800 newspapers and publications in America with Caglecartoons.com. His cartoons have appeared in *The New York Times*, *USA Today*, and *Time*, as well as on CNN, MSNBC, and *Fox News*. Additionally, his cartoons regularly appear on www.cagle.msnbc.com.

Brian is a native of Arizona and is married to the wonderful Stacey Heywood. They have three children who act like monkeys.

Fairrington (left) and Cagle (right) Portrait by Brian Fairrington.

Foreword by Dick Morris

Humor has always been a leavening agent in politics, making harsh and partisan commentary into funny and pithy satire. But in today's politics, humor is the sole remaining connection between civilized dialogue and the venom our politicians spew at one another.

So the collected cartoons Cagle has assembled are really the only safe way to take your dose of politics. If you take partisanship straight, it could prove hazardous to your health, but with a side of humor, it won't be so bad for you.

Some people will say that satire is redundant, given the ludicrous conduct of our elected officials. They have a point. But Cagle reaches deep down into their souls and finds something funny about them. For this, he deserves a Nobel Prize. But as there is none for humor, your buying this book will suffice.

Dick Morris was an adviser to Bill Clinton for 20 years; he is a *Fox News* analyst, bestselling author, and columnist for Cagle Cartoons, Inc. Dick Morris portrait by Taylor Jones.

About this book

The year saw controversies about movies (Brokeback Mountain and the DaVinci Code). Cartoonists flew into a frenzy when the Vice President shot a guy in the face. Celebrities were in the news, from Katie Couric taking over the anchor chair at the CBS Evening News, to Tom Cruise getting fired and Mel Gibson flying into a drunken, anti-Semitic rage. The war in Iraq continued with no end in sight; Israel invaded Lebanon and some notables passed away, including Serbian strongman Slobodan Milosovic, Crocodile Hunter Steve Irwin, Enron's Ken Lay and Al Qaeda's Al Zarqawi. It would be a good year for cartoonists, if not for the new pressures we were under from skittish editors after the Muhammad cartoons imbroglio.

We run the huge political cartoons web site at www.cagle.com. This book is the annual, paper version of our site, with collections of the best graphic commentary on all of the top news stories of the year, 2006 ... well, almost the year 2006. To get our book out at the end of the year, we "put it to bed" early, so our book is more like the best cartoons from November 2005 through the end of October 2006. We start with what may be the biggest reaction to cartoons ever, the violence in the Muslim world in response to the Danish Muhammad cartoons. We tell the story of how the controversy evolved, with commentary in words and pictures from many of the world's top editorial cartoonists. We end up with a similar Muslim reaction to remarks by Pope Benedict XVI.

All of the cartoonists in this book can be seen at www.cagle.com, with archives of their cartoons from recent years and, for most of their cartoonists, their e-mail addresses and links to their web sites. We think our site is the most widely used web site in Social Studies classrooms around the world. The most common e-mail we receive reads something like this: "Explain your cartoon to me, my essay about your cartoon is due tomorrow." Cartoonists like to think that they are hitting readers over the head with their blunt opinions, and the idea that students see our cartoons as "puzzles to be solved" is disappointing to cartoonists. Don't think of this book as a book of puzzles. This is a book of raw, shocking opinions, drawn to make readers react.

I regret that this book is sold in the humor section of the bookstore. Editorial cartoons can be funny, but more importantly, cartoons are a reflection of ourselves, our feelings and our reactions to the news of the day—a reflection that gives us a better view of who were and how we felt as history happened. This is a history book telling the story of 2006 with the clarity that can only be found in cartoons.

—Daryl Cagle

Artwork at left by Brian Fairrington

We Want to Hear from You!

As the reader of this book, *you* are our most important critic and commentator. We value your opinion and want to know what we're doing right, what we could do better, what areas you'd like to see us publish in, and any other words of wisdom you're willing to pass our way.

As an associate publisher for Que Publishing, I welcome your comments. You can email or write me directly to let me know what you did or didn't like about this book—as well as what we can do to make our books better.

Please note that I cannot help you with technical problems related to the topic of this book. We do have a User Services group, however, where I will forward specific technical questions related to the book.

When you write, please be sure to include this book's title and author as well as your name, e-mail address, and phone number. I will carefully review your comments and share them with the author and editors who worked on the book.

E-mail: feedback@quepublishing.com
Mail: Greg Wiegand
Associate Publisher
Que Publishing
800 East 96th Street
Indianapolis, IN 46240 USA

Reader Services

Visit our website and register this book at www.quepublishing.com/register for convenient access to any updates, downloads, or errata that might be available for this book.

The Danish Muhammad Cartoons

By Daryl Cagle

Nothing generates anger in the Muslim world like a cartoon. A cartoon-Jihad erupted in early 2006 after a Danish newspaper printed cartoons depicting the prophet Muhammad back in September 2005. Denmark's biggest newspaper, the *Jyllands-Posten,* was bombarded by street protests, international diplomatic controversy, and death threats against cartoonists who went into hiding, fearing for their lives. After the deaths of hundreds of protesters, our profession has been transformed; cartoons are no longer seen as trivial, but as powerful, and editors are newly timid about the potential blasts their cartoonist bomb-throwers can trigger.

Jyllands-Posten reporter Anders Raahauge wrote the following report to cartoonist Doug Marlette, who alerted me to the ongoing events before the cartoon-riots spread in January 2006:

To test the limits of self-censorship, we asked all Danish cartoonists to draw Muhammad. We were provoked by the fact that a Danish author of children's books couldn't find any illustrators for his planned, decidedly non-polemic book on the prophet. Twelve cartoonists dared. There has been a great uproar.

Five thousand Danish Muslims protested in the streets of Copenhagen; 12 Muslim ambassadors demanded that our Prime Minister should take immediate and harsh action against (us), which he firmly declined (to do). The ambassadors then complained to the "Organization of the Islamic Conference"; there has been a general strike in Kashmir, and a political party in Pakistan with Danish affiliations has put a bounty on the heads of the 12 Danish cartoonists: 50,000 Danish Kroners for each execution.

The newspaper ran the Muhammad drawings as part of an article about self-censorship in the press, noting that even with a free press defined by law, there are other constraints regarding what can be published. Muslim critics questioned the motives of *Jyllands-Posten* editor Flemming Rose, who commissioned the cartoons. Opponents claimed that the cartoons were printed only to incite Muslims. The paper was accused of being "right-wing" and "racist." Children's book author Kåre Bluitgen was accused of writing a book that was anti-Islam.

The Danish prime minister refused to meet with ambassadors from 11 Islamic countries, led by Egypt, who objected to Denmark's "smear campaign" and demanded punitive action against the newspaper. The ambassadors then announced a general boycott against Denmark. The United Nations weighed in, conveying sympathies to the offended Islamic countries and setting up a commission to seek retribution for the insults. Governments around the world condemned the cartoons.

To drum up anger in the Muslim world, some Muslims distributed other, much more offensive cartoons. The offices of the *Jyllands-Posten* and Danish embassies in various places around the world were repeatedly evacuated in response to bomb threats. Many nations joined in a boycott of Danish food products, imposing heavy costs on little Denmark.

Newspapers and magazines throughout Europe reprinted the cartoons, making a freedom-of-the-press argument in solidarity with the *Jyllands-Posten*. Some governments apologized for publications in their countries that reprinted the cartoons, while others closed newspapers that printed the cartoons. Some editors who dared to reprint the cartoons were fired, while some in the Middle East who dared to reprint the cartoons were jailed.

Riots continued for weeks worldwide, with crowds demanding the cartoonists be killed. Huge violent demonstrations in Nigeria, Pakistan, Libya, Turkey, Bangladesh, Iran, and Indonesia were repeated every day, each with tens of thousands of street protesters burning Danish flags, storming Western businesses, throwing stones, and chanting "death to America," even though America was not involved with the Danish cartoons. The death toll from the rioting grew steadily; in one cartoon riot in Nigeria, an estimated 138 people were killed.

A Muslim court in India sentenced the Danish cartoonists to death, and an Indian minister offered $10 million plus "the weight of the killer in gold" to anyone who would murder them. The cartoonists went into hiding, under police protection.

Anyone reading the majority of American newspapers that didn't reprint the cartoons would think the cartoons must be alarming, horrible insults. The cartoons must be seen to fully appreciate how banal and disappointing they really are. Very few of the protesters saw the cartoons. We have reprinted the offending cartoons in this book so our readers can judge for themselves.

Most Muslims consider any graphic depiction of Muhammad to be taboo. For the Muslim countries, it is a matter of imposing their own sensibilities upon the infidels in the West. For the Danish "infidels" at *Jyllands-Posten*, it is a matter of press freedom and an unwillingness to accept restrictions on an absolute and treasured freedom, which includes the right to offend anyone they choose.

Depictions of Muhammad are not the only cartoons that inspire Islamic rage. For years, there has been a great response to other cartoons that have insulted Muslims in a variety of ways. Montreal Gazette cartoonist Terry "Aislin" Mosher had a similar experience. Terry writes:

Margaret Thatcher once said that the two biggest dangers of the 21st century would be Islamic extremism and the Internet. One cartoon (opposite page) caused more reaction than any I have ever drawn, even if most of it was manufactured by a lobby group in Washington, D.C.

In November of 1997, a radical outfit calling itself the "Islamic Group" carried out the systematic torture and massacre of 60 harmless tourists in Luxor, Egypt. This is the most cowardly kind of act, and the horrible death of one small girl angered me in particular. Subsequently, I drew this cartoon of a clearly labeled Islamic extremist as a raving dog (understanding that this is considered an extreme insult in the Arab world, but not in ours—thus the apology to dogs).

The cartoon most certainly was not intended as an attack on the religion of Islam itself. Our new editorial page editor at The Gazette, *Peter Hadekel, flinched, but chose to print the cartoon anyway. There was no immediate reaction to the cartoons, most* Gazette *readers sharing my revulsion over the massacre. However, an outfit in Washington, D.C., named The Council on American-Islamic Relations (CAIR) whose job it is to monitor the portrayal of the Arab world closely in the North American Press, began a concentrated campaign against* The Gazette *and myself, demanding an apology several days after the cartoon appeared.*

Hadekel began receiving a ton of e-mail from around the world. One petition came from several hundred people of Arab descent in Fort Wayne, Indiana (where, of-course, the Montreal Gazette *is read closely every morning, I'm certain).*

A demonstration was held in front of The Gazette *replete with the burning of copies of the offending cartoon.* The Gazette *and Hadekel responded as best they could, by offering closer and more harmonious ties with Montreal's Arab communities. CAIR, it should be noted, is very hesitant in its denunciation of these massacres when they take place.*

A cartoonist whom I syndicate, Sandy Huffaker, drew a cartoon showing an Iraqi holding a book titled *Koran for Dummies*, as an American soldier asks, "Anything in there about GRATITUDE?" I was bombarded by many thousands of e-mails in a flame campaign instigated by CAIR, which asked readers on their website to e-mail me. The e-mails were hysterical, filled with colorful threats and demands that I fire and punish Huffaker. I posted a big batch of the e-mails on my website and asked my own readers to respond to CAIR. (My website has a rather large audience, so I flamed CAIR back.) Being on the other end of a flame campaign may have been a new experience for CAIR

because their flame campaign against me stopped abruptly—or, more likely, CAIR saw that the hysterical rantings of their supporters, displayed on my website, did not speak well for their cause.

Pulitzer Prize-winning cartoonist Doug Marlette of the *Tallahassee Democrat* found himself blasted by a CAIR e-mail-Jihad when he drew a cartoon with the caption, "What Would Muhammad Drive?" The drawing showed a man wearing Arab headdress and driving a Ryder truck (a reference to Oklahoma City bomber Timothy McVeigh). In response to an inquiry from *Jyllands-Posten*, Doug writes:

I was used to negative reactions from religious interest groups, but not the kind of sustained violent intensity of the Islamic threats. The nihilism and culture of death of a religion that sanctions suicide bombers and issues fatwas on people who draw funny pictures is certainly of a different order and fanatical magnitude than the protests of our home-grown religious true believers.

As a child of the segregated South, I am quite familiar with the damage done to the "good religious people" of my region when the Ku Klux Klan acted in our name. The CAIR organization that led the assault (on me) describes itself as a civil rights advocacy group. Among those whose "civil rights" they advocated were the convicted bombers of the World Trade Center in 1993. They cannot be taken seriously. For many of those who protested my cartoon, recent émigrés, many highly educated, it was obvious that there was not that healthy tradition of free inquiry, humor, and irreverence in their background that we have in the West. There was no Jefferson, Madison, Adams in their intellectual tradition. Those who have attacked my work, whether on the right, the left; Republican or Democrat; conservative or liberal; Protestant, Catholic, Jewish, or Muslim, all seem to experience comic or satirical irreverence as hostility and hate. When all it is, really, is irreverence. Ink on paper is only a thought, an idea. Such people fear ideas. Those who mistake themselves for the God they claim to worship tend to mistake irreverence for blasphemy.

Muslim countries expect the press in Denmark to suppress cartoons that would be offensive to them, but they don't extend the same cartoon courtesy to others that they demand for themselves. Cartoons in the Arab press are typically far more ugly and racist than anything American audiences have ever seen. Middle Eastern cartoon venom is targeted at Israel, often depicting Jews with hooked noses and orthodox garb, sometimes with bloody fangs, often in the roles of Nazis. The Jews are sometimes shown crucifying Arabs in a "Jews killed Jesus" scenario, or enacting their own concentration-camp Holocausts on their neighbors along with their henchmen, the Americans. The cartoons are designed to be as offensive as possible. Ironically, the Iranian government got a lot of publicity for sponsoring an anti-Semitic cartoon contest as a response to the Muhammad cartoons, even though Jews had nothing to do with the Muhammad cartoons—and even though anti-Semitic cartoons are everyday fare for Iranian newspaper readers.

Unless we defend our funny little drawings with the same zeal we see from the victims of our irreverence, we'll continue to see our freedoms constricted by the loud voices of those we offend.

—*Daryl Cagle*

These are the Cartoons...

Here are the 12 Danish cartoons that threw the world into a clash of civilizations...

The drawing of Muhammad with a bomb in his turban, by cartoonist Kurt Westergard, became the best-known of the controversial cartoons because it is easy to understand why Muslims would find it offensive. Many newspapers that were praised or condemned for printing the cartoons actually printed only this one cartoon. Fox News showed only this cartoon. Many newspapers referred to the cartoons as "The 12 Danish cartoons, including one of Muhammad with a bomb in his turban," giving the impression that all of the cartoons were as provocative as this one. Westergard was outspoken about the controversy, saying he has no regrets about the drawing: "I wanted to show that terrorists get their spiritual ammunition from Islam ... that does not mean that all Muslims are responsible for terror."

Claus Seidel

In contrast to the turban bomb, it is difficult to see why most of the drawings are offensive, aside from the notion of any depiction of Muhammad being offensive. The simple illustration by cartoonist Claus Seidel seems to be nothing more than a children's book illustration, with no hidden message.

Some of the cartoons are a comment about the assignment and the artist's attitude about drawing Muhammad. In this cartoon, Arne Sorensen shows that drawing the Prophet Muhammad can be intimidating.

Lars Refn didn't draw the Prophet Muhammad at all; he drew a schoolboy with a label saying that his name was "Muhammad." On the blackboard, the boy points to these words in Farsi: "The *Jyllands-Posten* journalists are a bunch of reactionary provocateurs." By being lumped in with the other cartoonists, Refn also had to go into hiding for his own safety, even though he did nothing more than criticize the *Jyllands-Posten*.

Cartoonist Bob Katzenelson drew a goofy caricature that is critical of Kåre Bluitgen, the self-promoting author who started the controversy when he couldn't find an illustrator who was willing to draw the Prophet Muhammad for his children's book. An orange labeled "PR Stunt" is falling into the Bluitgen's turban—Danes understand "an orange falling into your hat" as an idiom that means "good luck." The author is holding a stick-figure drawing of Muhammad, which would presumably bring him good luck through the crazy publicity he was seeking.

Annette Carlsen took another swipe at the publicity-seeking author Kåre Bluitgen in this cartoon, which shows a guy looking at a police lineup saying, "Hmmm ... I don't recognize him." Number seven in the lineup is Bluitgen, holding a little sign that reads, "Kåre's PR, call me, give me an offer." The guy looking through the one-way glass doesn't recognize Muhammad in the lineup, since no one knows what Muhammad looks like. It may be that Carlsen didn't include an image of Muhammad in this cartoon at all. It is a rule of thumb for cartoonists to put the gag at the right side of a cartoon, since we read from left to right, and the gag comes at the end; I see this as the cartoonist's intent to make Bluitgen the butt of the joke.

I see the drawing by editorial cartoonist Poul Erik Poulsen as the most insulting of the lot. Poul drew Muhammad with devil horns that seem to almost be a halo or crescent.

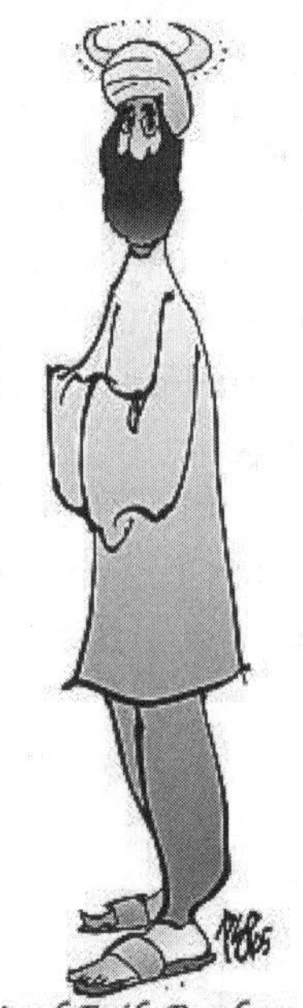

'oul Erik Poulsen

Rasmus Sand Hoyer's drawing is also quite provocative. Muhammad is shown in a menacing pose with a dagger, and he has a blindfold (or his eyes are "censored") in a graphic device that is the inverse or opposite of the eye slots of the two burqa-clad women behind him. It seems the artist is saying that Islam (or Muhammad) blindly threatens and suppresses women. Hoyer was reported to be a staff artist for the *Jyllands-Posten.*

This drawing by Peter Bungaard reminds me of the sketches a graphic artist makes when he is asked to create a corporate logo—but I don't see any message, gag, or point in combining the face with the symbol here.

This drawing by Franz Fuchsel shows a regal-looking guy, who may or may not be Muhammad, telling his angry guards something close to, "Relax, guys, it's just a drawing by some Dane from nowhere special."

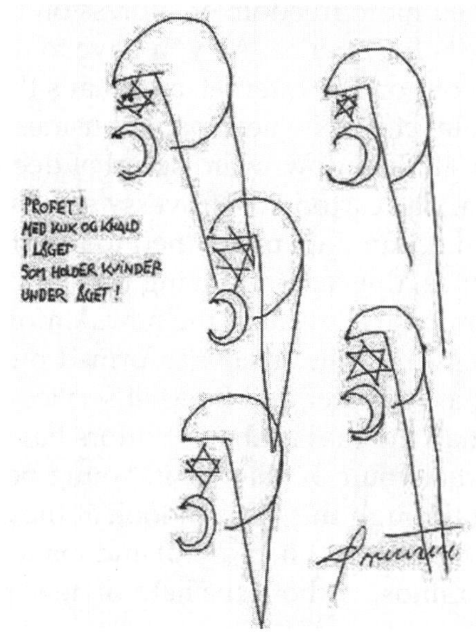

This drawing by Erik Abild Sorensen is a strange one. I don't see any depiction of Muhammad here. It seems to be another sketch from a graphic artist designing a logo on a napkin, this time including Jewish stars. In an excellent article in the June 2006 issue of *Harpers,* Art Spiegelman translates the rhyming text as: "Prophet, you crazy bloke! Keeping women under yoke!" This one doesn't make much sense.

Jens Julius Hansen is a regular contributor to our website, and his cartoons are featured in this book. Here Julius drew Muhammad greeting martyrs who believe that they will be rewarded with 72 virgins as they arrive in heaven. Muhammad says, "Stop! Stop! We have run out of virgins!"

Here's my Danish Muhammad Cartoon Scorecard. Out of 12 cartoons:
Six or seven have drawings of Muhammad;
Two show drawings of drawings of Muhammad;
Three likely do not show Muhammad at all;
Three are bashing the Jyllands-Posten *or the author, Bluitgen;*
And only three or four seem to have been drawn with the intent to be insulting or critical of the Prophet Muhammad.

Cartoonists on the Cartoons...

"Since the worldwide furor began over the Danish caricatures of Muhammad, the talk among political cartoonists has been about new and unwelcome attention the fuss has brought to their profession. Editors now view editorial cartoonists as potential problems, and gossip has circulated among American cartoonists about their cartoons that are being killed by timid editors and publishers who would have printed the same cartoons before the Danish Muhammad cartoon controversy. I asked a number of the world's top syndicated political cartoonists what they think about the 'toon turmoil' and how they see it affecting political cartoonists." —Daryl Cagle

Bob Englehart, *The Hartford Courant*:
"European newspaper cartoonists have always enjoyed more freedom of expression than we cartoonists in America. All you have to do is check them out on the Internet, and that's the real chill, the fatal chill. The newspaper business in America is caught in a downward spiral of declining circulation. The cartoon controversy shows why. Most all American papers declined to run the Danish cartoons, thus again proving that newspapers are becoming irrelevant to the news/information process. You, the curious informed public, need to have a computer and Internet service to learn what all the fuss is about. Editors have decided for you that you can't handle it. Young people see right through this. They'll look at the cartoons on the Internet (as I had to do) and make up their own minds, without the help of newspapers."

Sandy Huffaker, Cagle Cartoons:
"When a chain buys a newspaper, that paper loses courage. The money guys take over for the journalists, leading to the firing of reporters, investigative reporters, and cartoonists—those people who might upset advertisers. It seems like one letter-to-the-editor can cow an editor already afraid for his job. No better example of this is the Muhammad cartoons. Only a handful of our papers had the guts to run them, so no one had any idea how offensive they were or weren't (they were quite tame). I never thought I'd see the day that France, who had a number of papers run the cartoons, had more courage than we did. It is a sad day for democracy."

Mike Lester, *The Rome News-Tribune,* Georgia: "Methinks the temptation for timidity in the opinions of editors and cartoonists has never seen greater justification. For cartoonists, the previous desire to appear in major papers and newsstand glossies seems to have been replaced by the desire to maintain their current height. I'm not sure who the last brave editor will be, but he/she's out there. I once drew a cartoon of Jesus turning regular into decaf and was deluged with mail from Christians requesting T-shirt reprints. It would appear that, even though the West has been watching *Skating with Celebrities* and smoking Sudafed, we've somehow developed a sense of irony leaving the Dark-Aged, Islamo-fascists still working on indoor plumbing and a sense of humor."

Rainer Hachfeld, *Neues Deutschland,* Germany: "Editors are and were always timid, particularly in the USA. Nothing will change in the behavior of editors. On the other hand, I hate the ridiculous self-pity of cartoonists which is shown in many cartoons about the so-called Muhammad cartoon controversy."

Yaakov Kirschen, *The Jerusalem Post,* Israel: "Timid editors do indeed avoid 'hard-hitting' cartoons. Timid editors are also partially responsible for falling newspaper sales because when newspapers choose to be 'safe' rather than exciting, provocative, and thought-provoking they lose their appeal. And nothing is more exciting, provocative, and thought-provoking than a good political cartoon."

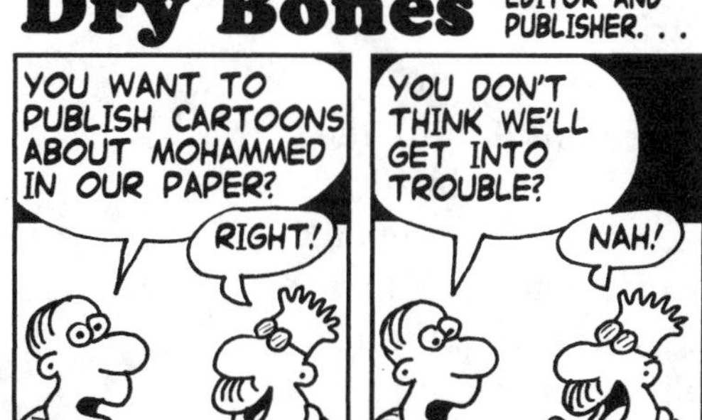

Mike Lane, Baltimore, Cagle Cartoons:
"Newspaper people I've known, editors included, were generally divided unevenly into two groups: pro- and anti-cartoon. So why we should expect editors to even consider (printing) foreign cartoons of an inflammatory nature when many could not care less about comparatively benign, domestic cartoons is a mystery to me. And if the Muslims are going to get worked up over cartoons of a guy who's been dead for 1,500 years when we've been drawing images of Jesus, who preceded Muhammad by 600 or so years, I say, okay, it's your way, not mine. So let's have a separation of church/temple/mosque and the Fourth Estate. If we're going to get exercised about what pictures our free press doesn't print, I say it should be over the photos of our dead and maimed young people returning from Iraq."

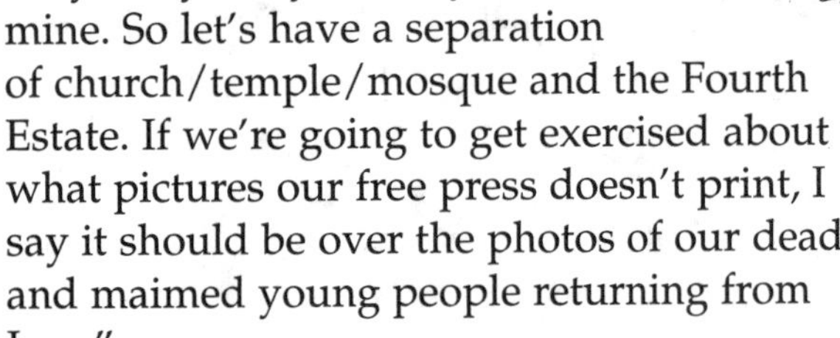

Petar Pismetrovic, ***Kleine Zeitung,*** **Austria:**
"I have no idea why anyone needed such cartoons. I think the goal of cartoons is not to insult, but to criticize, ape, or comment on politics, society, etc. As if there weren't enough sinners walking the earth (politicians, military leaders, etc.) that saints and religious idols needed to be attacked in cartoons. My only wish is that cartoons stop being misused by extremist organizations and elements, and that they are appreciated for what they should be: critical comment and a good joke."

Olle Johansson, *Norra Vasterbotten,* Sweden: "The upside to the incident with the Danish Muhammad cartoons is that I believe many editors will open their eyes to the immense power that is within the political cartoon. The downside is that, at the same time, many of them may unfortunately choose a more careful approach, especially when it comes to international cartoons concerning people and/or cultures they don't fully understand. But I choose to believe that this will strengthen the cartoon as journalistic instrument. And it has certainly brought back the nerve to this form of art."

Riber Hansson, *Svenska Dagbladet,* Sweden: "In Swedish children's books, you can find 'the world's strongest girl,' Pippi Longstocking. She used to say, 'If you are very, very strong, you have to be very, very kind.' A political cartoonist supported by [a free press] will be very, very strong. You can immediately see the dilemma for an artist trying to follow Pippi's advice; the political satirist's basic tool is not exactly kindness. My personal policy as an editorial cartoonist is to [strike only at] power. Belief belongs to the private sphere, and I try to avoid religious subjects for that reason. I can't guess what my reaction would have been if my courage as a cartoonist had been challenged, as it was with the Danish cartoonists by editors asking [them to] dare draw the Prophet Mohammad. Self-censorship is an emotive and provoking term for a political cartoonist, maybe for all artists. I hope I would have had the courage to say 'no.' The political cartoon needs to be free, without any editorial finger over the cartoonist's shoulder, pointing out the subject [matter]."

Patrick Chappatte, *International Herald-Tribune*, Geneva:
"I'm bothered by the fact that in the Danish approach, Muhammad was not merely a cartoon character, but he was the very purpose of the cartoons. The idea was to represent him because he's a forbidden figure. On the other side, those images have been misused by extremists to stir up anger and misunderstanding [by] the same extremists who take delight in anti-Semitic caricatures. The aim of political cartooning is not—should not be—in itself to hurt; it is to make a point. It can be a political or a moral point. It can be funny or serious. In the process, it can hurt your feelings, your political beliefs, or your religious principles—but this is a collateral damage. Muhammad is not a subject. Violent radical Islamists are a subject. Humiliation of the Palestinian people is a subject."

Vince O'Farrell, *The Illawarra Mercury*, Australia:

"To deliberately antagonize the Muslim community, especially in the context of broader world events, was an irresponsible exercise in abuse of freedom of the press. The response from the rampaging fanatical zealots was just as stupid and pathetic. Who'd want to be the head of the Islamic Public Relations Bureau? Now there's a 24/7 job. In almost 30 years of newspaper cartooning, I could probably count the number of times I've had a definite 'NO' from an editor to a cartoon on one hand. As newspaper publishing the world over is increasingly driven by the bottom line, cartoonists in general will have to expect that those 'hard-hitting' cartoons, especially the ones that go after the corporate juggernauts, etc., will more and more be assigned to the wastepaper or 'too hard basket.'"

Pat Bagley, *The Salt Lake Tribune*, Utah:

"The Muhammad brouhaha has probably strengthened my hand when it comes to arguing for printing a cartoon that the editors might find a little too edgy, especially those dealing with religion. The episode has opened the door on why religion is somehow exempt from criticism. Wasn't that the whole point of The Enlightenment, that folks could speak back to religious authority?"

A View from Jordan

Our Jordanian cartoonist, Emad Hajjaj, wrote to me with his views of the cartoon furor and included a cartoon that his newspaper refused to print (right).

" ابغض بغيضك هوناً ما ، عسى ان يكون حبيبك يوماً ما "
" إنما الشديد من يملك نفسه ساعة الغضب "
صدق رسول الحلم والاعتدال عليه افضل الصلاة والسلام
UNPUBLISHED
لا للعنف والفوضائية وتهديد حياة الأبرياء وتكريس الصورة السلبية عن المسلمين
نعم للمقاطعة التجارية والرد الدبلوماسي والاعلامي وكافة وسائل الاحتجاج الحضارية
www.mahjoob.com

Daryl,

Recently, I followed your blog on the daily coverage of the controversial Mohammad cartoon crisis. I appreciate the great effort that you do in giving different perspectives about this important issue. I would like to share my thoughts on this.

Everyone has the right to freedom of expression. However, there can be consequences for expressing those rights. For example, no one can make fun of the race of blacks or Jews and not expect some backlash. The difference in doing this in the West is that you are not forbidden from doing it, but you may experience some retaliation and negative feedback. The idea of forbidding the drawing of Muhammad is just a historical dogma. The Koran and Hadeeth never mention in any clear text that the depiction of Muhammad is forbidden. But there is a difference between Islam and Muslims, who are unfortunately, a Third World people with many distorted beliefs and thoughts about their own religion, their own history, and the world itself. I think that a billion and a half Muslims deserve to be understood rather than be provoked or hit on their nerve under the pretext of freedom of expression that serves no purpose.

Muhammad has been portrayed in cartoons and comics for decades in the West, and in a very miserable way long before the Danish newspaper published them. The difference this time was that *Jyllands-Posten* was putting it in this bold way: "Hey, Muslims, you forbid it, but we'll publish it anyway." They went ahead and published 12 cartoons that depicted a negative image of Muhammad. Our embarrassed dictatorships who could not do anything about Abu-Ghraib and Fallouja (as the official defenders of Islam!) found something to play with in this golden chance crisis. Who is Denmark to them, anyway? It is not the United States. So they urged our controlled media to exaggerate the issue and encourage protests and boycotts. In doing this, they indirectly encouraged our religious cleric extremists to get even more crazy. The timing could not have been worse for all Muslims—but our puppet leaders won this image battle and looked liked heroes of Islam!

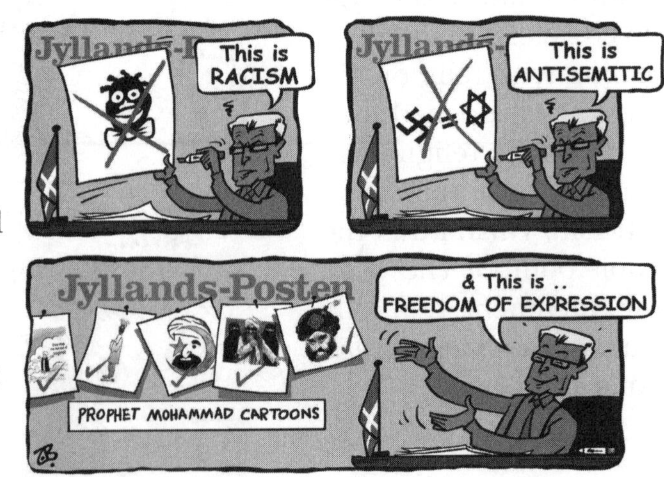

The United States and Europe are living in the age of Islamo-phobia. The Muslims think they became the only target of the whole West, and these cartoons are just making it worse. Muslims are human beings, after all, and what they deserve from the West is more understanding and more support for the few positive things they have. Give them democracy, but not like the one in Iraq. Stop your governments and big companies from playing dangerous games in our region. Use the money you spend on weapons and spend it on education and fighting poverty, illiteracy, and unemployment in Islamic countries. Then I'm sure there will be no terrorists or religious freaks anymore. When you keep practicing your freedom of expression in this manner, you will only get more hate and more extremism, and give proof to the Bin Laden vision.

The clash of civilizations is the last thing our troubled planet needs, if such a clash is really happening. We should not encourage it because nobody will win after it happens. Finally, talking about Arabic cartooning, yes, it has a lot of negative things, like anti-Semitism, racism, and many awful things. However, it is changing just like many things here; what the Danish newspaper did, did not help in that change.

Attached is a recent cartoon of mine (opposite page, top) that urges all Muslims to be civilized in their protest and stop the looting and burning. Unfortunately, the two Arabic newspapers I work for refuse to publish it. I'm telling you this just to prove that extremism in the West (even if it was for a noble cause like freedom of expression) feeds Islamic extremism (fighting freedom of expression under the pretext of defending Islam!).

—Emad Hajjaj

Flemming Rose, the culture editor for the *Jyllands-Posten* who commissioned the caricatures of Muhammad, wrote a long, interesting piece in the *Washington Post* that ran in newspapers around the world; here are some excerpts:

… I commissioned the cartoons in response to several incidents of self-censorship in Europe caused by widening fears and feelings of intimidation in dealing with issues related to Islam. And I still believe that this is a topic that we Europeans must confront, challenging moderate Muslims to speak out. The idea wasn't to provoke gratuitously—and we certainly didn't intend to trigger violent demonstrations throughout the Muslim world. Our goal was simply to push back self-imposed limits on expression that seemed to be closing in tighter.

At the end of September, a Danish standup comedian said in an interview with Jyllands-Posten *that he had no problem urinating on the Bible in front of a camera, but he dared not do the same thing with the Koran.…*

… Around the same time, the Tate gallery in London withdrew an installation by the avant-garde artist John Latham depicting the Koran, Bible and Talmud torn to pieces. The museum explained that it did not want to stir things up after the London bombings. (A few months earlier, to avoid offending Muslims, a museum in Goteborg, Sweden, had removed a painting with a sexual motif and a quotation from the Koran.)

Finally, at the end of September, Danish Prime Minister Anders Fogh Rasmussen met with a group of imams, one of whom called on the prime minister to interfere with the press in order to get more positive coverage of Islam.

So, over two weeks we witnessed a half-dozen cases of self-censorship, pitting freedom of speech against the fear of confronting issues about Islam. This was a legitimate news story to cover, and Jyllands-Posten *decided to do it by adopting the well-known journalistic principle: Show, don't tell. I wrote to members of the association of Danish cartoonists asking them "to draw Muhammad as you see him." We certainly did not ask them to make fun of the prophet. Twelve out of 25 active members responded.…*

… When I visit a mosque, I show my respect by taking off my shoes. I follow the customs, just as I do in a church, synagogue or other holy place. But if a believer demands that I, as a nonbeliever, observe his taboos in the public domain, he is not asking for my respect, but for my submission. And that is incompatible with a secular democracy.…

… I acknowledge that some people have been offended by the publication of the cartoons, and Jyllands-Posten *has apologized for that. But we cannot apologize for our right to publish material, even offensive material. You cannot edit a newspaper if you are paralyzed by worries about every possible insult.…*

Political Cartoonists vs. Illustrators

By Daryl Cagle

Why did the Danish cartoonists draw the cartoons? To test the limits of press freedom? To show disrespect for Islam? Because a Danish author couldn't find an illustrator for his book about Muhammad? No, the Danish cartoonists drew "caricatures" of Muhammad because a Danish newspaper, the *Jyllands-Posten,* hired them and paid them $73 each, along with the promise that the cartoonists would get their names and artwork in the local newspaper.

The cartoonists knew they were being hired to draw provocative cartoons accompanying an article about the limits on press freedom, but they had no idea they would be the tiny spark to light a huge bomb in the Muslim world. (If they had known, they certainly wouldn't have done the drawings in exchange for getting their names in the newspaper.)

As condemnation pummeled the Danish cartoonists, an important distinction was lost: the difference between cartoonists who are illustrators and those who are political cartoonists. I'm a political cartoonist; I draw cartoons that convey my opinions. Anyone who sees my cartoons will know what I think on a wide range of issues. Political cartoonists are journalists; like columnists, we decide for ourselves what we want to say, and we are responsible for what we say. Editors don't tell political cartoonists what to draw (although editors sometimes stop us from saying things that are too offensive).

The Danish cartoonists were drawing as illustrators; they were given assignments by clients who paid them for their work. Illustrators draw what they are hired to draw. No one can look at the work of an illustrator and discern what the illustrator's opinions are. Illustrators usually draw pictures that go with an author's words; they might be creative and inject their own ideas, but they are still working at the direction of a client. The Muhammad cartoons are not political cartoons: they are illustrations drawn to accompany a newspaper article about press limits, an issue that arose because a self-promoting author couldn't find an illustrator for his book about Muhammad.

The Danish Muhammad cartoons are broadly—and wrongly—described as political cartoons by pundits and politicians who don't understand the difference between one kind of cartoonist and another. The "political cartoon" label unfairly condemns the Danish cartoonists, none of whom would have chosen on their own to express any opinion about Islam, press freedom, or the Prophet Muhammad. The perception of the Danish Muhammad cartoons as "political cartoons" is chilling to real political cartoonists, who are suddenly perceived as ticking time-bombs that can explode at any time. Editors, who were already uncomfortable reining in their unwieldy, bomb-throwing cartoonists, are now more timid than ever. Regrettably, the Danish Muhammad illustrations and the resulting world turmoil have done more to reshape the political cartoonists' profession than any other single event.

Everyone asks me why I don't draw Muhammad in a political cartoon: am I afraid to give offense or am I afraid for my own safety? I'll draw whatever I want; I'll be offensive if I want to be, but I want my cartoons to effectively convey my opinion, and my opinion about the Danish Muhammad cartoons issue is that the violent response to the cartoons was wrong and was far out of proportion to the provocation. If I were to draw a cartoon depicting Muhammad now, the only message the cartoon would convey is, "Hey, look at me, I can offend you, too." That is not what I choose to say.

—Daryl Cagle

ABDUL ALWAYS KNEW HOW TO IMPRESS THE GIRLS.

Why Cartoons Still Matter ... a LOT

By Scott Stantis

While rioting packs of Muslim men in Afghanistan, Syria, and Iran shout "Death to cartoonists," newspapers in the United States have been doing exactly that for years with lay-offs, buyouts, firings, and dropping cartoons from the editorial pages.

Altogether, the ranks of American full-time staff editorial cartoonists has shrunk from a high of more than 200 in the 1980s to less than 80 today.

Newspapers with a long and storied history of cartoonists have seen fit to cut loose this valuable resource. Papers such as the *Los Angeles Times* and the *Baltimore Sun* are now without a staff cartoonist. *The Chicago Tribune* recently dedicated a room honoring the late great cartoonist Jeff MacNelly, while at the same time mocking his legacy by leaving the editorial cartoonist position open since his death in June 2000.

These same newspapers now go days without running any cartoon in their opinion sections. Presumably, the editors believe that nothing attracts and engages readers better than massive stretches of gray type.

And the cartoons that do find their way into print are more often jokes then commentary. Guy Cooper, former editor of the popular "Perspective" section in *Newsweek* magazine, told a gathering of editorial cartoonists that he would never run a hard-hitting, substantive editorial cartoon on his page. He viewed them strictly as entertainment. The *New York Times*, which runs a small number of editorial cartoons in its Sunday "Week-In-Review" section, has recently renamed the collection "Laugh Lines."

Cartoons can show an issue in high-definition clarity better than any 10,000 words. It's interesting to note that when the editors of the Danish newspaper *Jyllands-Posten* decided to deride Europe for not confronting the issue of growing radical Islamism, they chose to do so with cartoons.

I won't pass judgment on the decision of whether to run the Muhammad cartoons, other than to say they were drawn solely to provoke. And provocation for its own sake is immature and a waste of the valuable real estate given to cartoonists' work by newspapers.

Having said that, it's important to note that great cartoons provoke thoughtful and passionate debate—the good ones, anyway. If we're doing our job right, we engage the readers. In an age when publishers are terrified of losing a single one of their remaining subscribers, the angry call from a reader canceling his subscription because of today's editorial page cartoon is not a welcome reader response.

HORSEMEN OF THE APOCALYPSE

Editors may think that cartoons are irrelevant, but people don't. A good cartoon can get you in your gut and make you double over in pain or laughter.

Happily, there are still a handful of newspapers (the *Birmingham News* being chief among them) that believe in the mission of engaging cartoons.

From the beginning of our republic, cartoons have challenged and provoked, from Benjamin Franklin's dismembered snake with each individual colony's name on each piece and the caption " Join or die," to Thomas Nast's dismembering of the corrupt Tweed Ring in 19th-century New York City. Cartoons also define an issue and even make caricatures of real flesh and blood politicians. Herblock and Pogo diminishing Joseph McCarthy. Or Herblock's rendering of Richard Nixon emerging from under a sewer cap. Jeff MacNelly drawing a hapless Jimmy Carter buying the Brooklyn Bridge from the Soviet Union. These cartoons left an indelible mark on history.

Talk of relevance, or lack thereof, has been grinding on the editorial cartoon profession for years. In fact, in 2002, the year I served as president of the Association of American Editorial Cartoonists, I had a panel address the issue, "Do we matter?"

To answer this question, editors might ask themselves: Do you think the streets of the Arab world would be ablaze if that Danish newspaper had run a series of editorials on the same subject as those cartoons?

Scott Stantis is the political cartoonist for the *Birmingham* (AL) *News* and the creator of the comic strip, *Prickly City*.

ALEN LAUZAN FALCON
Chile

MICHAEL RAMIREZ
Investors Business Daily

ISLAMIC EXTREMISM

WE CAN'T THINK OF ANYTHING MORE OFFENSIVE TO THE MUSLIM COMMUNITY THAN CARTOONS OF MUHAMMED.

AND THAT'S THE PROBLEM....

NICK ANDERSON
Houston Chronicle

OLLE JOHANSSON
Sweden

ETTA HULME
Ft. Worth Star Telegram

THAT'S OFFENSIVE !

CARTOON

THAT'S ACCEPTABLE !

LONDON

EXTREME VIEW

PAUL ZANETTI
Australia

ZANETTI .NET .AU

M.e. COHEN

DON WRIGHT
Palm Beach Post

PAVEL CONSTANTIN
Romania

IdiotBOX Matt Bors

IT'S NOT A WAR THEY WANTED, BUT IT CAME TO THEIR SHORES WITH THE PUBLICATION OF THE MUHAMMAD CARTOONS ON **SEPTEMBER 30, 2005**, A DAY THAT CHANGED HISTORY.

RADICAL LEADERS ARE TAKING ADVANTAGE OF PEOPLE'S FEAR, WHIPPING THEM INTO A **NATIONALIST, RACIST** FERVOR.

A **MILLION DOLLAR** BOUNTY HAS BEEN PLACED ON THE HEADS OF THE CARTOONISTS.

THEY'VE EVEN GONE SO FAR AS TO **RENAME DANISH PASTRIES***

*TRUE!

NO DOUBT THIS INCIDENT WILL BE USED TO JUSTIFY ALL TYPES OF VIOLENCE AND **INSANE, REPRESSIVE** POLICIES FOR YEARS TO COME.

IT'S ALL SO... **AMERICAN** OF THEM!

MATT BORS
Idiot Box

ERIC ALLIE
Politicalcartoons.com

VINCE O'FARRELL, Illawarra Mercury, Australia

KIRK ANDERSON

ALEN LAUZAN FALCON, Chile

IN AN ATTEMPT TO SOOTHE EMOTIONS OVER RECENT CARTOON EVENTS, WE'VE DECIDED TO PUBLISH THIS IMAGE OF A CUTE PUPPY. WE TRUST THIS MIGHT HELP US ALL REMEMBER THE IMPORTANT THINGS IN LIFE...

CAMERON CARDOW, Ottawa Citizen

BRIAN FAIRRINGTON, Cagle Cartoons

BILL SCHORR

JEFF STAHLER
Columbus Dispatch

THOMAS "TAB" BOLDT
Calgary Sun (Canada)

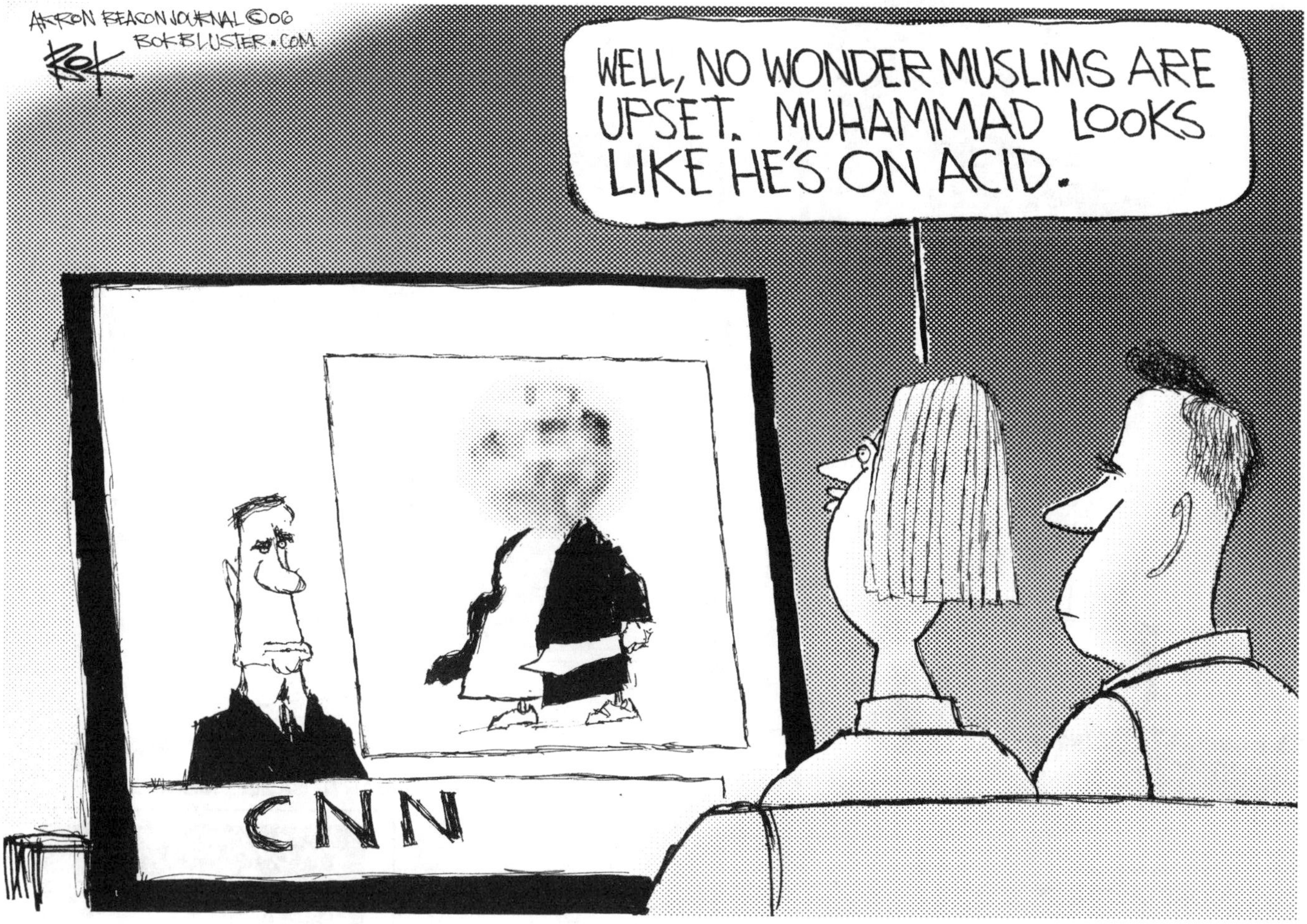

AKRON BEACON JOURNAL ©06
BOKBLUSTER.COM
BOK

WELL, NO WONDER MUSLIMS ARE UPSET. MUHAMMAD LOOKS LIKE HE'S ON ACID.

CNN

CHIP BOK, Akron Beacon Journal

OSMANI SIMANCA
Brazil

AND FINALLY, A CARTOON THAT OFFENDS NO ONE...

JEFF KOTERBA, Omaha World Herald

CAMERON CARDOW
Ottawa Citizen
Canada

DARYL CAGLE, MSNBC.com

PAVEL CONSTANTIN
Romania

WAYNE STAYSKAL, Tribune Media Services

EMAD HAJJAJ Jordan

DARIO CASTILLEJOS, Mexico

LAILSON de HOLLANDA, Brazil (below and below right)

The Pope's Remarks

Pope Benedict XVI made controversial remarks quoting a Byzantine emperor who said Islam was a violent religion. The Catholic Church immediately began damage control—but while the pope apologized, some cartoonists pointed out that sometimes the truth hurts.

JENS
JULIUS
HANSEN
Denmark

M.e. COHEN
Politicalcartoons.com

GARY BROOKINS
Richmond Times-Dispatch

MIKE KEEFE
Denver Post

JEFF KOTERBA, Omaha World Herald

DOUG MARLETTE
Tulsa World

SANDY HUFFAKER, Cagle Cartoons

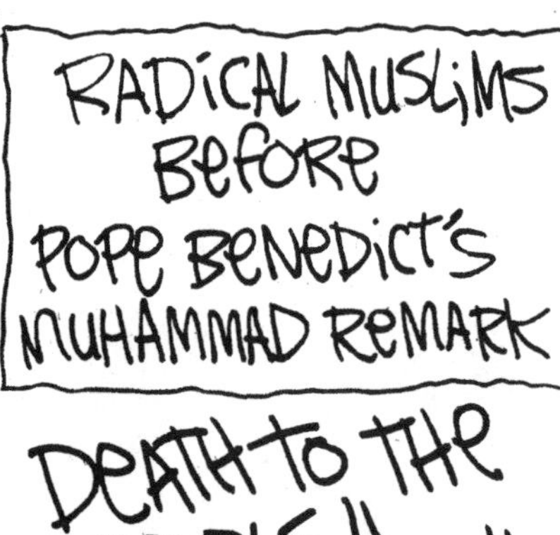

GARY McCOY, Cagle Cartoons

STEVE BREEN
San Diego
Union Tribune

PAUL ZANETTI, Australia

MICHAEL RAMIREZ
Investors Business Daily

DICK LOCHER, Chicago Tribune

PAVEL CONSTANTIN
Romania

MIKE LANE
Cagle Cartoons

TERRY (AISLIN) MOSHER, Montreal Gazette

EMAD HAJJAJ
Jordan

DANA SUMMERS
Orlando Sentinal

NICK ANDERSON
Houston Chronicle

DON WRIGHT
Palm Beach Post

THE POPE AS A DANISH CARTOONIST

PATRICK CHAPPATTE, International Herald Tribune

CHUCK ASAY
Colorado Springs Gazette

MIKE LESTER
Rome News-Tribune (GA)

BOB GORRELL

FREDERICK DELIGNE
Nice-Matin, France

DARYL CAGLE
MSNBC.com

YAAKOV KIRSCHEN
Dry Bones
Jerusalem Post
Israel

BRIAN FAIRRINGTON
Cagle Cartoons

Brokeback Mountain

"Oh give me a home where the buffalo roam where the deer and the antelope are gay..."

Director Ang Lee turned the classic star-crossed lovers romantic formula on its head with the film *Brokeback Mountain*, or what quickly became widely known as "the gay cowboy movie." No other film was so critically praised and lambasted. Supporters commended Brokeback's challenge of the status quo, while conservative religious groups and *Fox News* said the film was an example of Hollywood pushing political agendas. Brokeback received eight Oscar nominations, more than any other film, and won three awards at the March ceremony. And all year it had critics and champions alike quoting protagonist Jack Twist's (Jake Gyllenhaal) tag-line plea to lover Ennis (Heath Ledger): "I wish I knew how to quit you."

BRIAN FAIRRINGTON
Cagle Cartoons

GRONDAHL
STANDARD-EXAMINER

CONGRESS

LOBBYISTS

BROKEBACK MOUNTAIN

CAL GRONDAHL
Utah Standard Examiner

ROBERT ARIAIL
The State (SC)

VINCE O'FARRELL
Illawarra Mercury
Australia

DARYL CAGLE
MSNBC.com

BOB ENGLEHART, Hartford Courant

MILT
PRIGGEE

BROKEBACK MOUNTAIN

MIKE KEEFE
The Denver Post

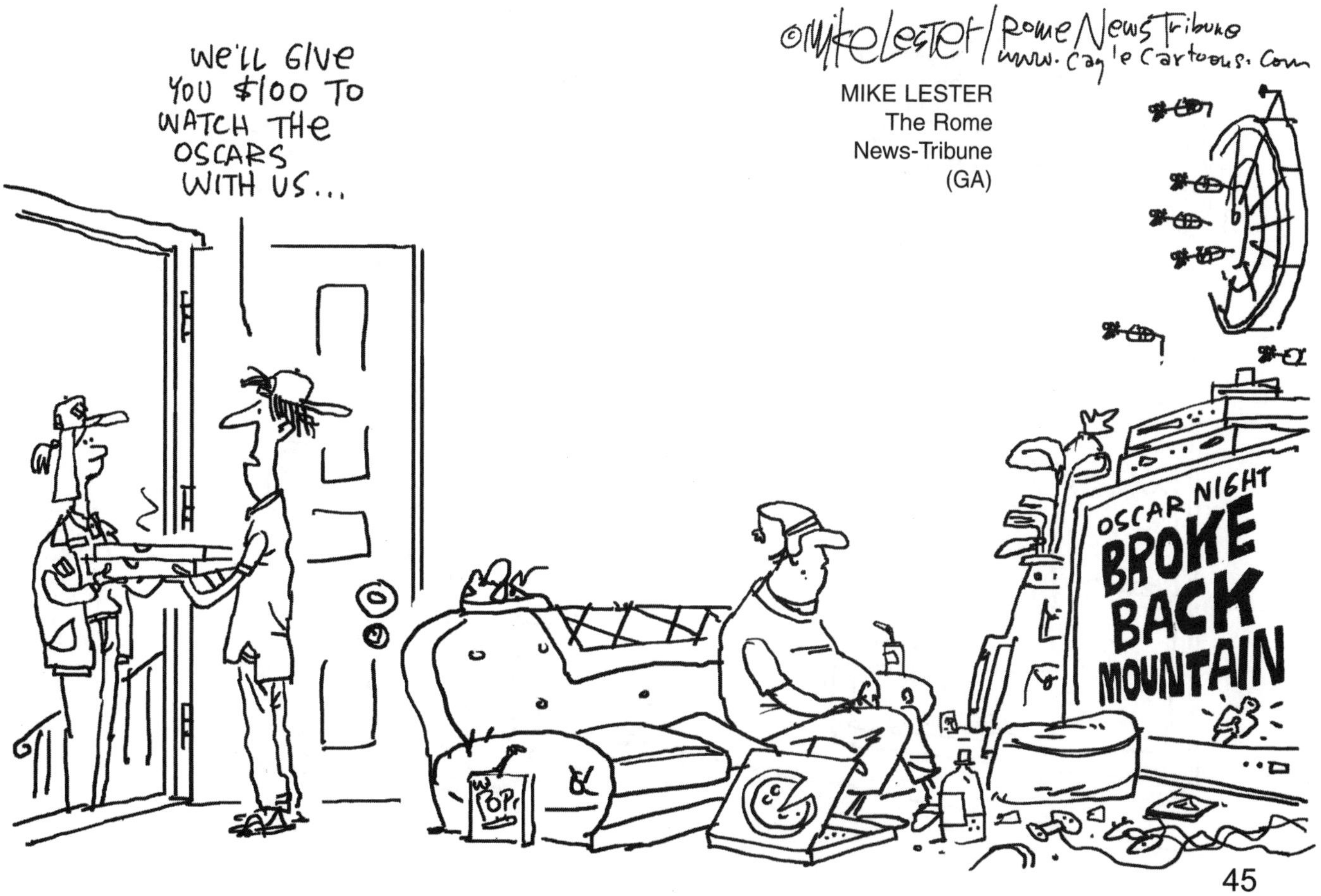

MIKE LESTER
The Rome
News-Tribune
(GA)

LARRY WRIGHT
The Detroit News (MI)

CINE
NOW PLAYING
BROKEBAC
MOUNTAI

...MY MOM AND DAD WENT TO THE MOVIES LAST NIGHT AND TODAY THEY THREW AWAY MY COWBOY HAT AND TOY SIX-GUNS.

WEIRD.

©2005
LARRY WRIGHT
THE DETROIT NEWS

caglecartoons.com

BROKEBACK MOUNTAIN
SOLD OUT

SO I GUESS THAT MEANS...

EVERY SEAT IS FILLED.

DON'T SAY IT.

© MIKE LESTER/www.caglecartoons.com

BROKEBACK MOUNTAIN

PAUL ZANETTI
Australia

BROKEBACK CAPITOL HILL

YOU DANCE WITH THEM THAT BRUNG YOU, CONGRESSMAN!

GOD, I WISH I KNEW HOW TO QUIT YOU!

LOBBYIST

1/25 2006 DARKOW COLUMBIA DAILY TRIBUNE

MIKE LESTER
The Rome
News-Tribune (GA)

JOHN DARKOW
The Columbia
Daily Tribune, MO

I DIDN'T KNOW HARRY WAS GAY.

Immigration

The House and Senate argued about immigration rules as Republicans were split. President Bush's friendly approach would allow illegal immigrants a path to citizenship; hardliners in the House opposed Bush's "amnesty." There was a fiery debate across the country, from Congress to street protests to editorial cartoons. Finally, a bill was passed to build a fence along about seven hundred miles of the border.

CAL GRONDAHL, Utah Standard Examiner

"So, you wish to enter legally? Great, you're the first in line."

SHENEMAN The Star-Ledger

DREW SHENEMAN
Newark Star-Ledger

"IT SAYS THIS ORANGE JUICE IS MADE WITH FRUIT PICKED ENTIRELY BY AMERICAN WORKERS. IT'S 43 DOLLARS."

DARYL CAGLE
MSNBC.com

MEXICAN BORDER

ILLEGAL IMMIGRANTS

RANDY BISH
Pittsburgh Tribune-Review

ANY LUCK IN CONTROLLING THE LEAK?

MATT DAVIES
Journal News
(NY)

DARIO
CASTILLEJOS
Mexico

NATE BEELER
Washington Examiner

KEEP OUT

THEY SAY BEHIND THIS WALL LIES THE LAND OF FREEDOM AND OPPORTUNITY...

©2006 The Examiner
nbeeler@dcexaminer.com

DARIO
CASTILLEJOS
Mexico

DAVID HORSEY, Seattle Post Intelligencer

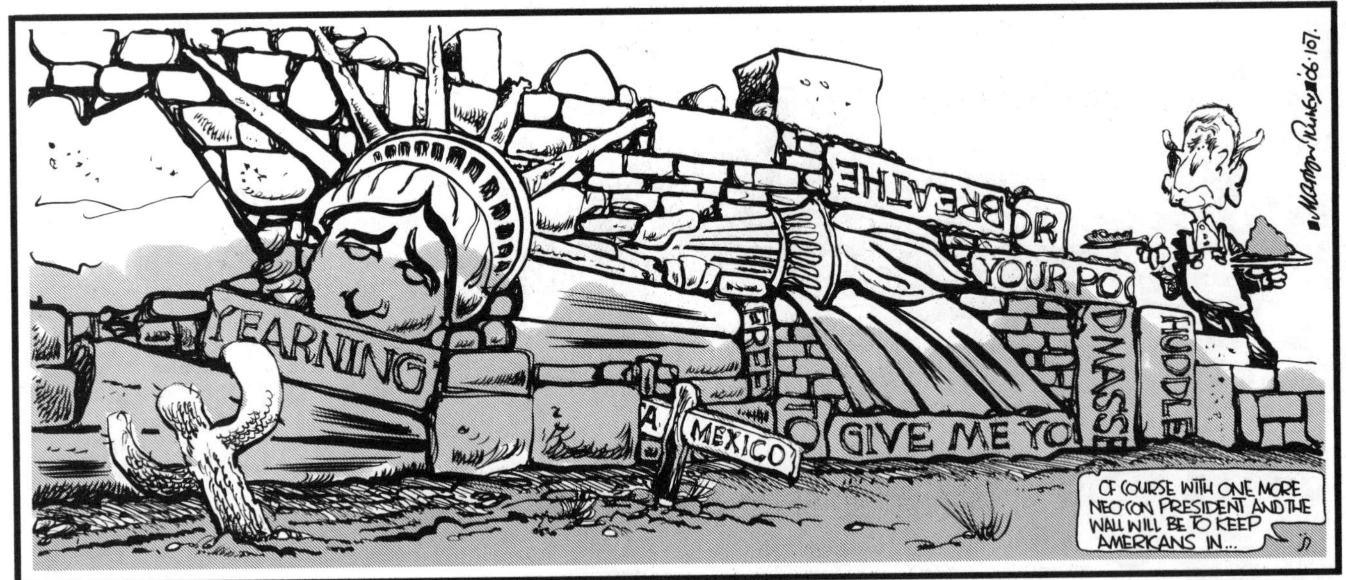

YEARNING
MEXICO
GIVE ME YO
BREATHE
OR
HUDDLE
OF COURSE WITH ONE MORE NEO-CON PRESIDENT AND THE WALL WILL BE TO KEEP AMERICANS IN...
MARTYN TURNER, Irish Times

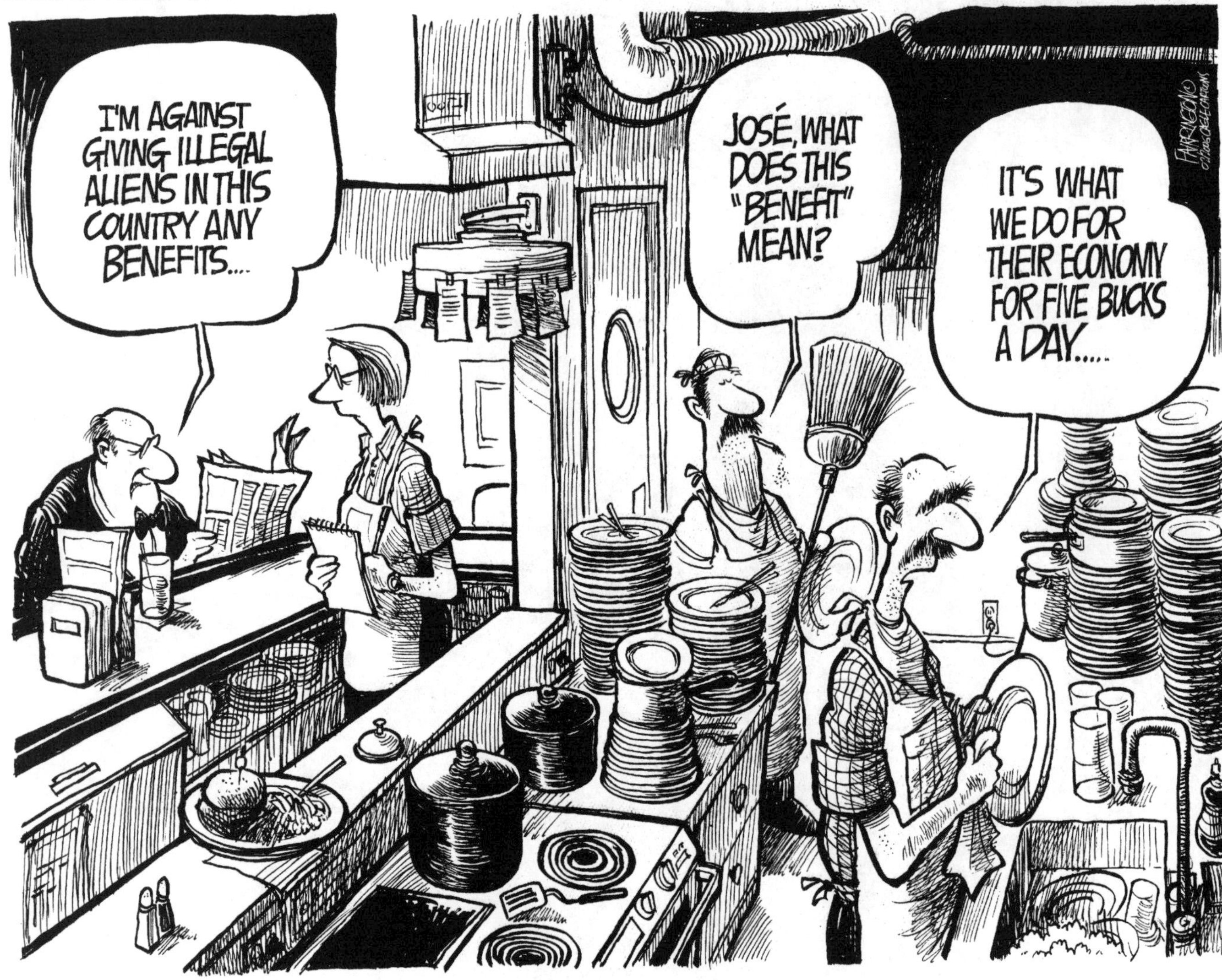
I'M AGAINST GIVING ILLEGAL ALIENS IN THIS COUNTRY ANY BENEFITS....
JOSÉ, WHAT DOES THIS "BENEFIT" MEAN?
IT'S WHAT WE DO FOR THEIR ECONOMY FOR FIVE BUCKS A DAY.....
BRIAN FAIRRINGTON, Cagle Cartoons

ROGELIO NARANJO, El Universal, Mexico

FREDERICK DELIGNE, Nice-Matin, France

PAUL COMBS, Tampa Tribune

JEFF KOTERBA, Omaha World Herald

MIKE LESTER, Rome News Tribune

DARIO CASTILLEJOS, Mexico

JOHN COLE
Scranton Times Tribune

MIKE KEEFE
Denver Post

DARYL CAGLE
MSNBC.com

ARES
Cuba

ARES.

BILL DAY
Memphis
Commercial
Appeal

NICK ANDERSON
Houston Chronicle

Katie Couric

The *CBS Evening News*, suffering in last place, and Katie Couric, bubbly long-time co-host of NBC's *Today Show*: a match made in television, apparently. This September, Couric took over as anchor of the *CBS Evening News*, following in the footsteps of greats such as Dan Rather, Walter Cronkite, and Edward R. Murrow. Cartoonists reminded the public that Couric is well versed in entertainment and short skirts, not serious reporting.

DARYL CAGLE, MSNBC.com

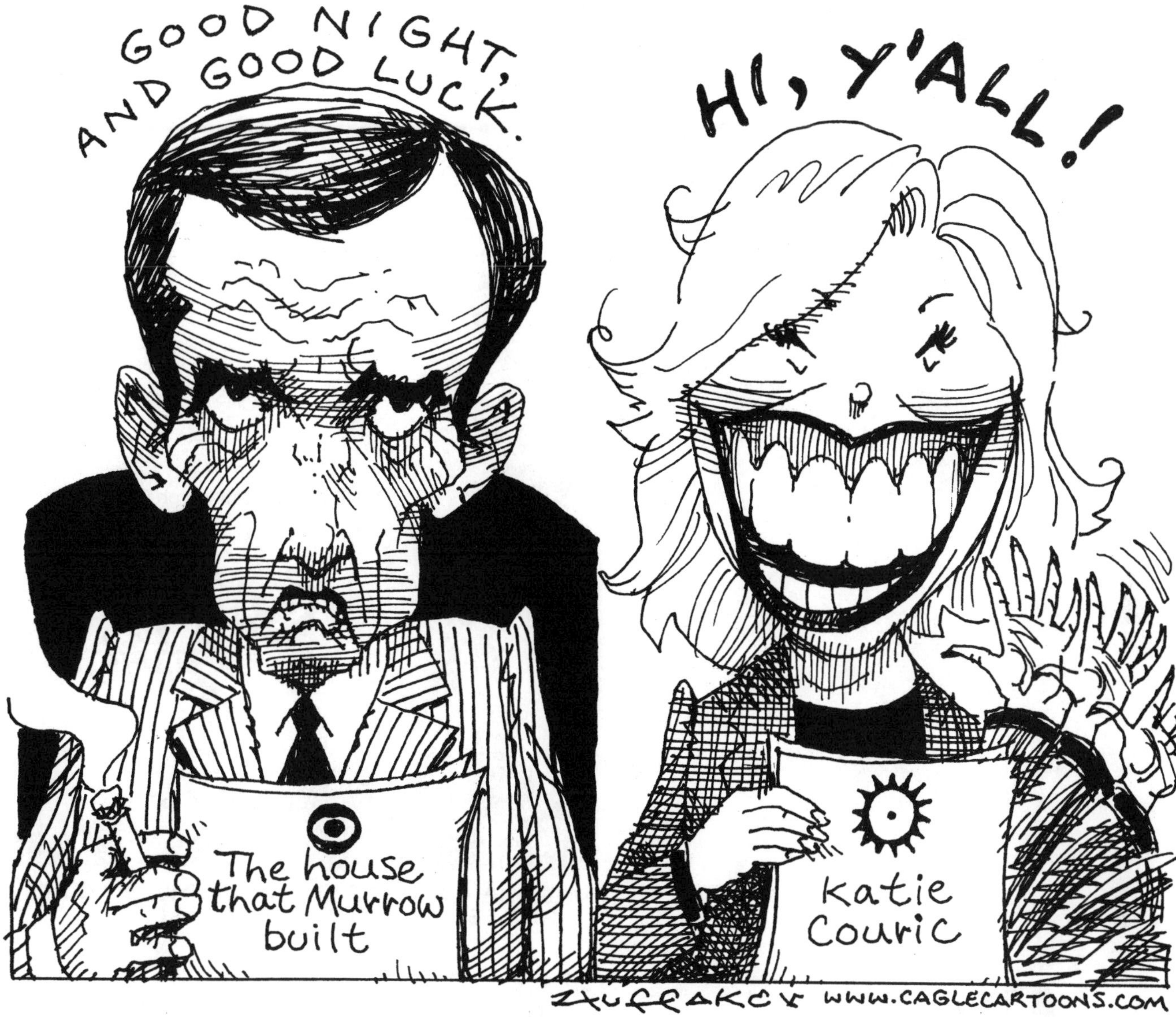
GOOD NIGHT, AND GOOD LUCK.
HI, Y'ALL!
The house that Murrow built
Katie Couric
HUFFAKER WWW.CAGLECARTOONS.COM

SANDY HUFFAKER, Cagle Cartoons

WOW! THAT GUY'S A LITTLE OLD TO BE DOING BACKFLIPS! WHO IS HE?
BOB SCHIEFFER.
KATIE TO CBS

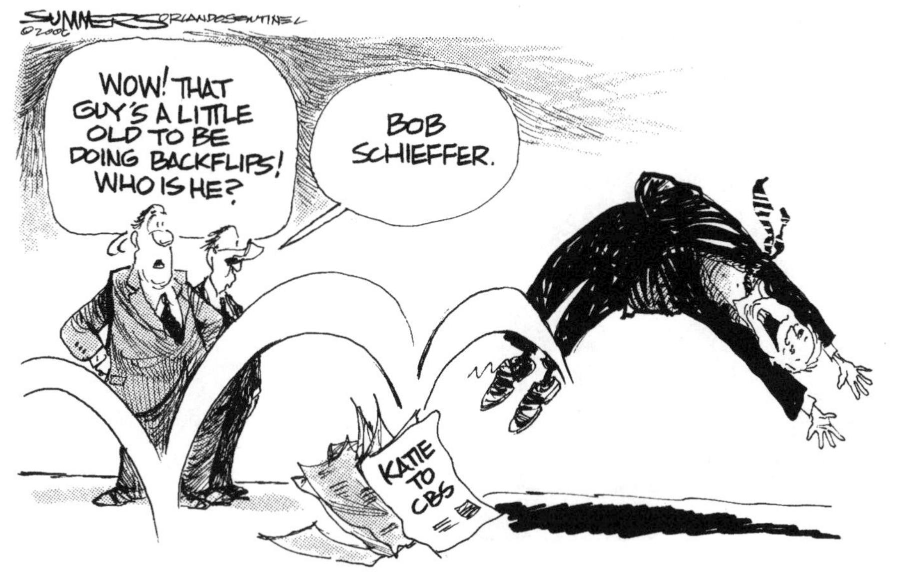

DANA SUMMERS
Orlando Sentinel

The Evolution of CBS NEWS

GARY VARVEL, Indianapolis Star

RANDY BISH, Pittsburgh Tribune-Review

WE USED TO BE CBS, BUT EVER SINCE WE HIRED KATIE COURIC WE'VE BEEN JUST "TOO DARNED PERKY"

JOHN DARKOW
The Columbia Daily Tribune (MO)

STEVE BREEN, San Diego Union-Tribune

GARY MARKSTEIN

DOUG MARLETTE, Tulsa World

ROB ROGERS
Pittsburgh Post-Gazette

MIKE LESTER
Rome News-Tribune (GA)

KATIE COURIC CBS NEWS ANCHOR DEBUT : THE MORNING AFTER...

IS IT ME, OR DOES EVERYBODY SEEM, -I DON'T KNOW... "PERKIER"?

©MIKE LESTER / ROME NEWS TRIBUNE
www.caglecartoons.com

CHIP BOK, Akron Beacon-Journal

GARY BROOKINS, Richmond Times-Dispatch

KEN CATALINO

"OK, ENOUGH ABOUT THE VATICAN—WHATCHA THINK OF MY NEW DESIGNER PUMPS?"

LARRY WRIGHT, Detroit News

JOHN COLE, Scranton Times-Tribune

STEVE KELLEY
New Orleans Times-Picayune

GARY McCOY
Illinois Business Journal

The DaVinci Code

Author Dan Brown's best-selling novel *The Da Vinci Code* infuriated Christians with its Jesus-married-Mary Magdalene storyline even before it was made into a blockbuster film starring Tom Hanks. Angry religious groups called Code blasphemous and staged popular protests. While revitalized churches filled more pews than theaters did seats for Code, cartoonists tried to remind the public that the film was a work of fiction.

MICHAEL RAMIREZ
Investors Business Daily

WHY THE MONA LISA IS SMILING

VINCE O'FARRELL
Illawarra Mercury
Australia

DREW SHENEMAN
Newark Star-Ledger

OMAHA WORLD-HERALD
KOTERBA
WITH THESE PRICES, I'M CONVINCED MORE THAN EVER OF HIDDEN CHARGES AND COMPLICATED OIL COMPANY CONSPIRACIES!!
SOMEONE'S A BIT TOO INVOLVED IN THE DA VINCI CODE...
PAY AT THE PUMP
GAS 'n' GIT

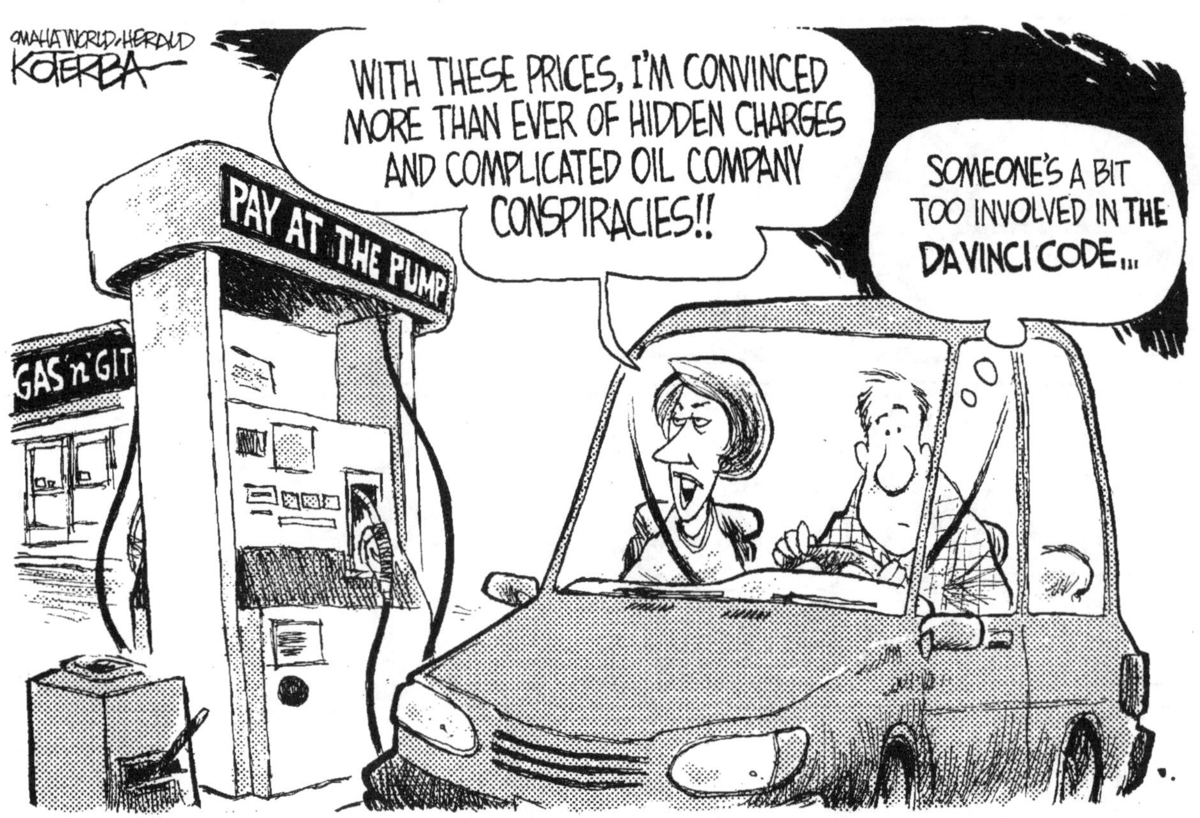

JEFF KOTERBA, Omaha World Herald

MIKE KEEFE, Denver Post

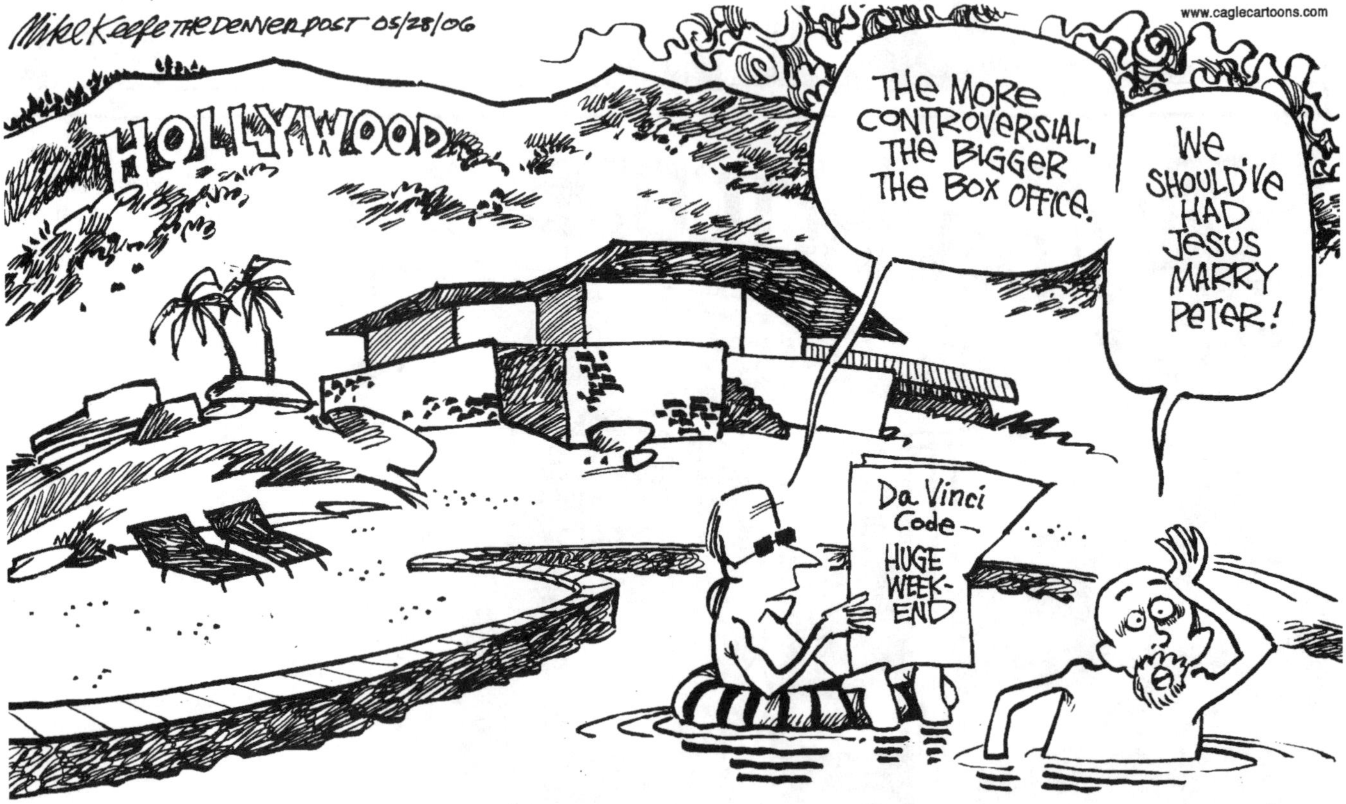
Mike Keefe THE DENVER POST 05/28/06
www.caglecartoons.com
HOLLYWOOD
The More CONTROVERSIAL, The Bigger The Box office.
We Should've HAD JeSUS MARRY PeTeR!
Da Vinci Code — HUGE WEEK-END

NATE BEELER, Washington Examiner

VINCE O'FARRELL
Illawarra Mercury, Australia

JEFF STAHLER, Columbus Dispatch

NOW SHOWING: THE DA VINCI CODE

HOW MANY TICKETS, SIR?

TICKETS

manfrancisco@yahoo.com

MANNY FRANCISCO
Manila, Phillipines

ROB ROGERS
Pittsburgh Post-Gazette

PATRICK CHAPPATTE
International Herald Tribune

DANA SUMMERS
Orlando Sentinel

NATE BEELER
Washington Examiner

WAYNE STAYSKAL
Tribune Media Services

DAVID HORSEY
Seattle Post Intelligencer

CHIP BOK
Akron Beacon-Journal

PAUL ZANETTI
Australia

STEVE BREEN
San Diego Union-Tribune

Mona Lisa's smile explained

STEVE NEASE
Oakville Beaver, Canada

Ann Coulter

Ann Coulter always says crazy, offensive things, but this year she said some especially crazy, offensive things, accusing 9/11 widows of being uncaring profiteers. Cartoonists love crazy and offensive—and they sure love to bash Ann Coulter.

TAYLOR JONES
Tribune Media
Services

Jim Day, Las Vegas Review-Journal

CHRISTO KOMARNITSKI
Bulgaria

JIMMY MARGULIES
The Record (NJ)

JACK OHMAN
Portland Oregonian

JOHN SHERFFIUS
Boulder Daily Camera

caglecartoons.com ©MATSON THE NEW YORK OBSERVER

DOES ANN COULTER FALLING ALONE IN THE FOREST MAKE A SOUND?

R.J. MATSON, St. Louis Post-Dispatch

SANDY HUFFAKER
Cagle Cartoons

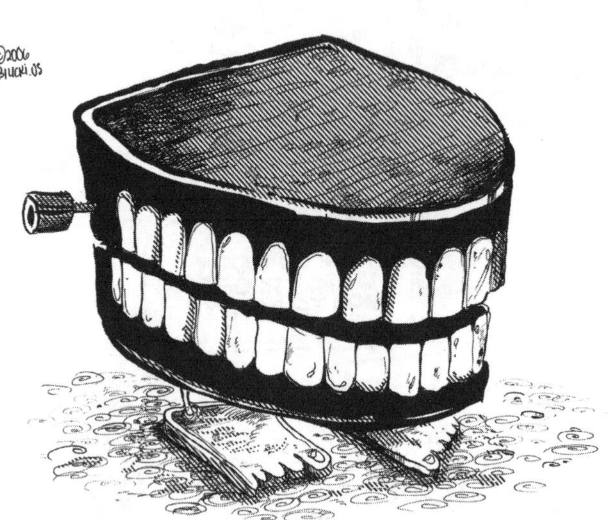

ANN COULTER
(DRAWN TO SCALE)

JUSTIN BILICKI

CHRIS BRITT
State Journal-Register (IL)

JOHN DEERING, Arkansas Democrat Gazette

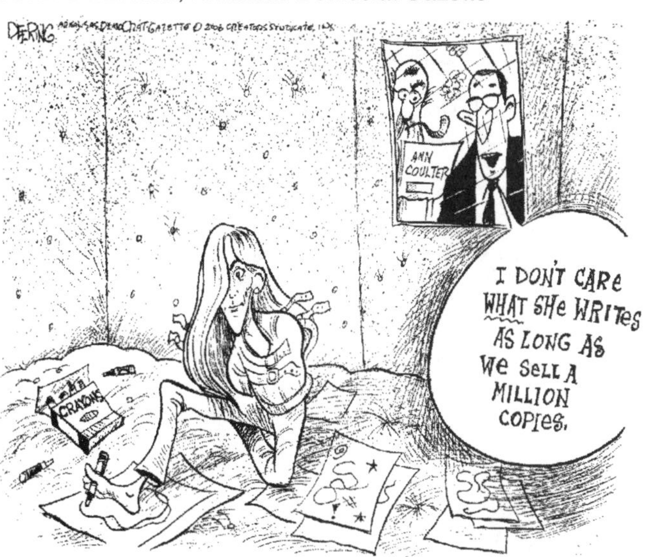

MIKE KEEFE, Denver Post

FELIPE THE TERRIBLY ACCEPTING SHOW POODLE AFTER SNIFFING ANN COULTER'S REAR.

AMMO

MR. FISH

DWAYNE BOOTH
MR. FISH

LARRY WRIGHT, Detroit News

THE DETROIT NEWS
LARRY WRIGHT
©2006

EMBARRASS ANN COULTER!

IT GETS BORING AFTER AWHILE. SHE HITS THE BULLSEYE EVERY TIME.

caglecartoons.com

MIKE LESTER
Rome News-Tribune (GA)

THE 9-11 JERSEY GIRLS

BOB ENGLEHART
Hartford Courant

The Ann Coulter Collection
At Christmas
Anybody Who's Not a Christian Should Be Shot!
Ho! Ho! Ho!
What are you laughing about you liberal scum!
Peace On Earth
After We Nuke Iran and Korea

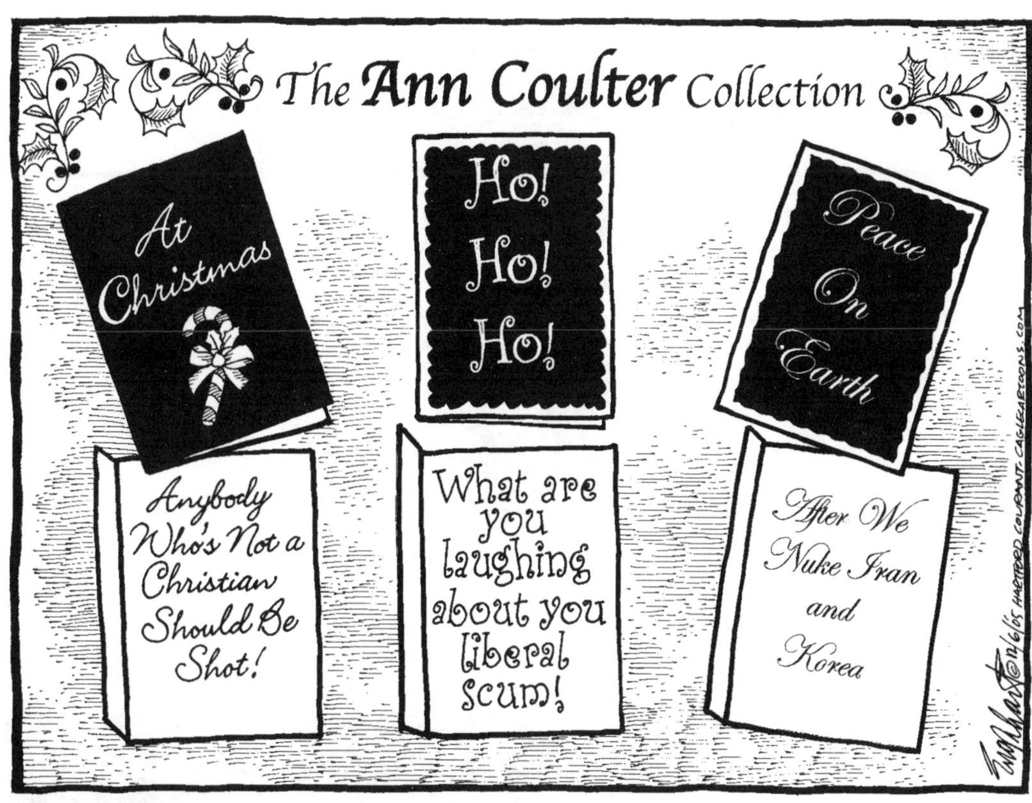

MONTE
WOLVERTON
Cagle Cartoons

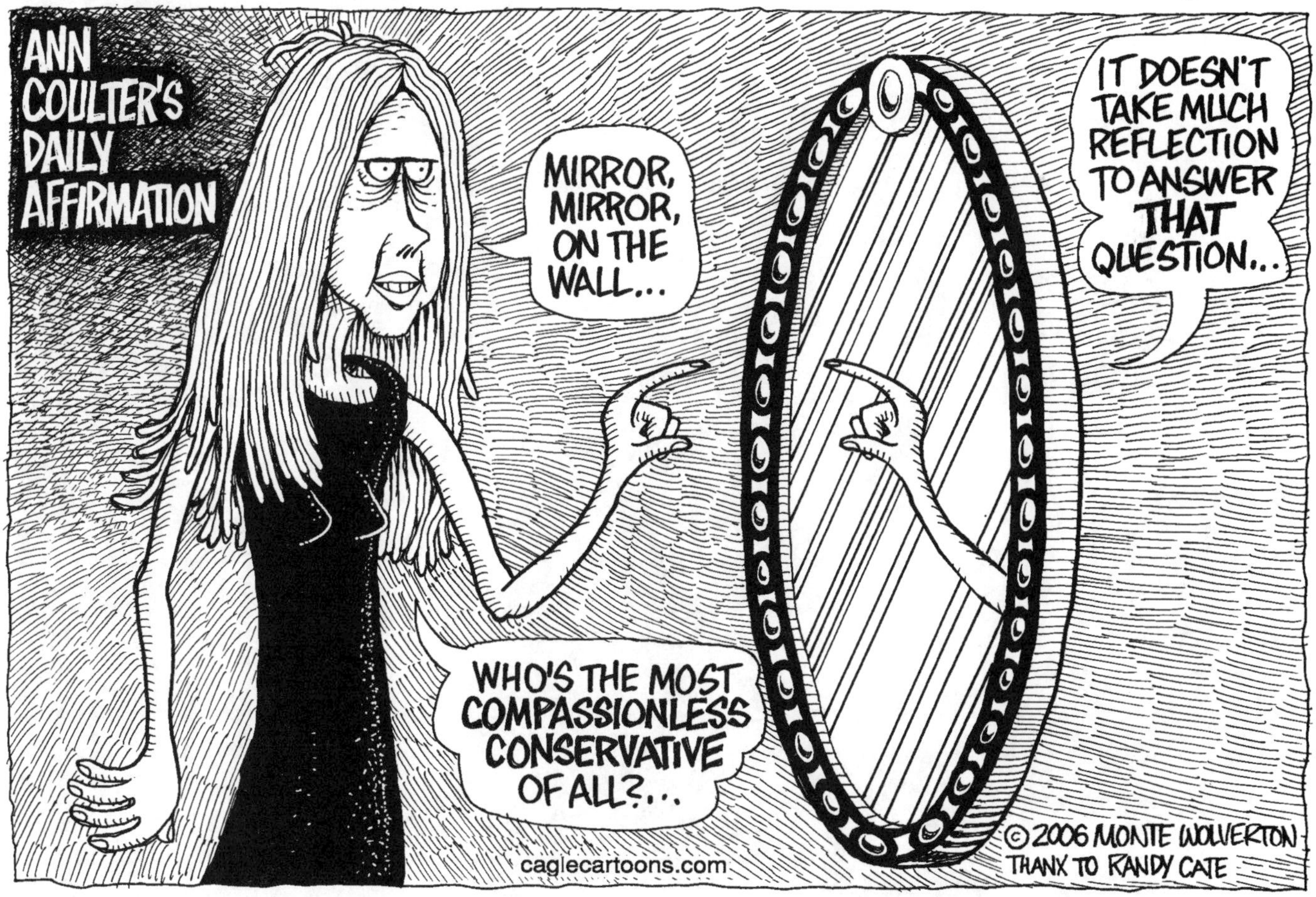
ANN COULTER'S DAILY AFFIRMATION
MIRROR, MIRROR, ON THE WALL...
WHO'S THE MOST COMPASSIONLESS CONSERVATIVE OF ALL?...
IT DOESN'T TAKE MUCH REFLECTION TO ANSWER THAT QUESTION...
© 2006 MONTE WOLVERTON
THANX TO RANDY CATE
caglecartoons.com

STEVE BENSON
Arizona Republic

WHICH IS WITCH?
9/11 WIDOWS
ANN COULTER

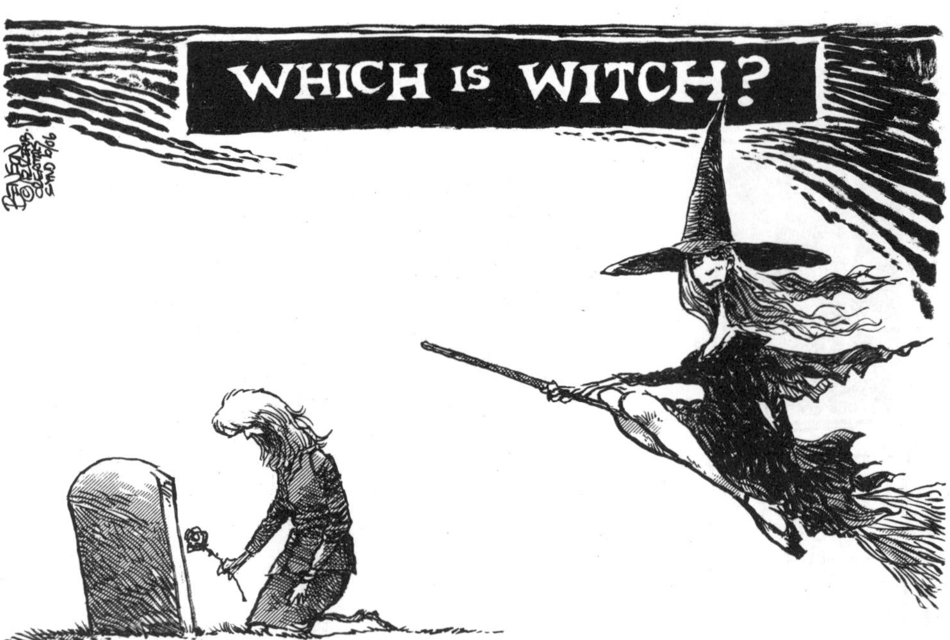

STEVE SACK
Minneapolis Star Tribune

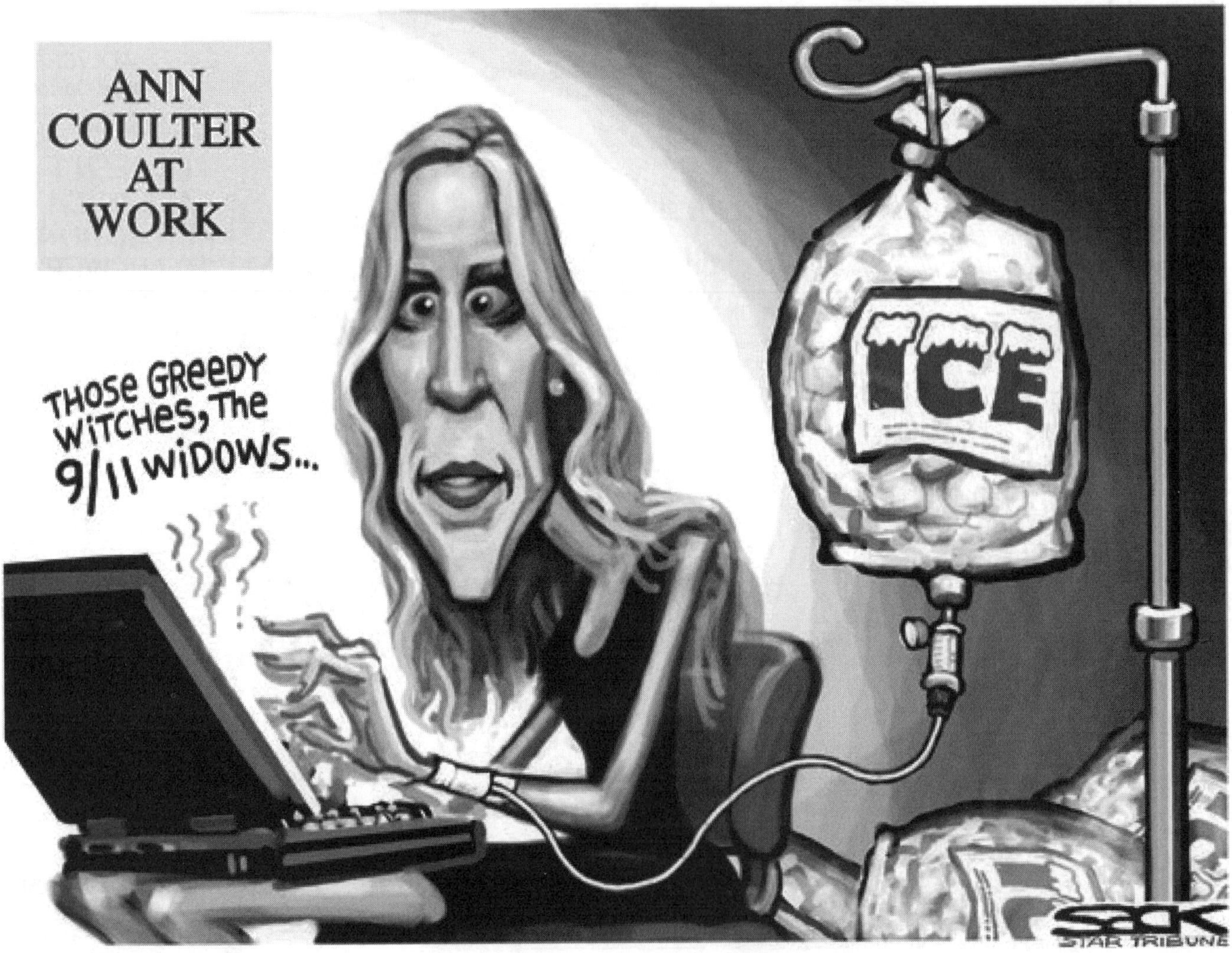
ANN COULTER AT WORK
THOSE GREEDY WITCHES, THE 9/11 WIDOWS...
ICE
SACK
STAR TRIBUNE

TROUBLETOWN IT MUST BE SWEEPS WEEK

BY LLOYD DANGLE

THE WIVES OF 9-11 VICTIMS ARE GODLESS WHORES!

YOU KNOW WHAT I CALL FOUR-STAR GENERALS WHO CRITICIZE THE WAR PLAN?

DICKLESS LIBERALS.

HEE HEE!

WHEN HENRY THE EIGHTH WAS PRESIDENT OF ENGLAND, HE'D CHOP OFF ANYBODY'S HEAD WHO CRITICIZED HIS PRESIDENCY.

THAT'S DEMOCRACY.

LLOYD DANGLE
Troubletown

Mel Gibson

Mel Gibson has always seemed a little off, but this year we all got confirmation. When Gibson was caught driving drunk in Malibu this summer, he blamed the Jews for "all the wars in the world" and referred to one of his female arresting officers as "sugar tits." He later apologized for his comments and checked into rehab. Editorial cartoonists didn't want Gibson's wild ride to end.

PETER LEWIS
Newcastle Herald
Australia

SCHORR 2006
UNITED FEATURE SYN

BILL SCHORR

"OUR ORDERS ARE TO EXPAND THE MILITARY CAMPAIGN AND BOMB MEL GIBSON'S HOUSE..."

HENRY PAYNE
Detroit News

R.J. MATSON, The New York Observer

PATRICK O'CONNOR
Los Angeles Daily News

GARY MCCOY, Cagle Cartoons

GARY VARVEL, Indianapolis Star

J.D. CROWE, Mobile Register

MIKE KEEFE, Denver Post

MIKE GRASTON, Windsor Star

PETER NICHOLSON, The Australian, Sydney

HOLYG#W!

What kind of reaction are you hearing around town to Mel Gibson?

MARGULIES
© 2006 THE RECORD NEW JERSEY
www.northjersey.com/margulies

JIMMY MARGULIES, The Record (NJ)

DAN WASSERMAN, Boston Globe

NIK SCOTT, Australia

Step away from the cross, Mr Gibson

MOVIE POSTERS REVISITED...

#@☆💀 JEWS!!!
JEWS!!
☆#@*!
☆#@☆
💀!
MAD MAX
1979

TEQUILA SUNRISE
1988

signs
2002

8/3 ©2006 THE BUFFALO NEWS WWW.ADAMZYGLIS.COM ADAM ZYGLIS

ADAM ZYGLIS, Buffalo News

ED STEIN, Rocky Mountain News

LARRY WRIGHT, Detroit News

MICHAEL RAMIREZ
Investors Business Daily

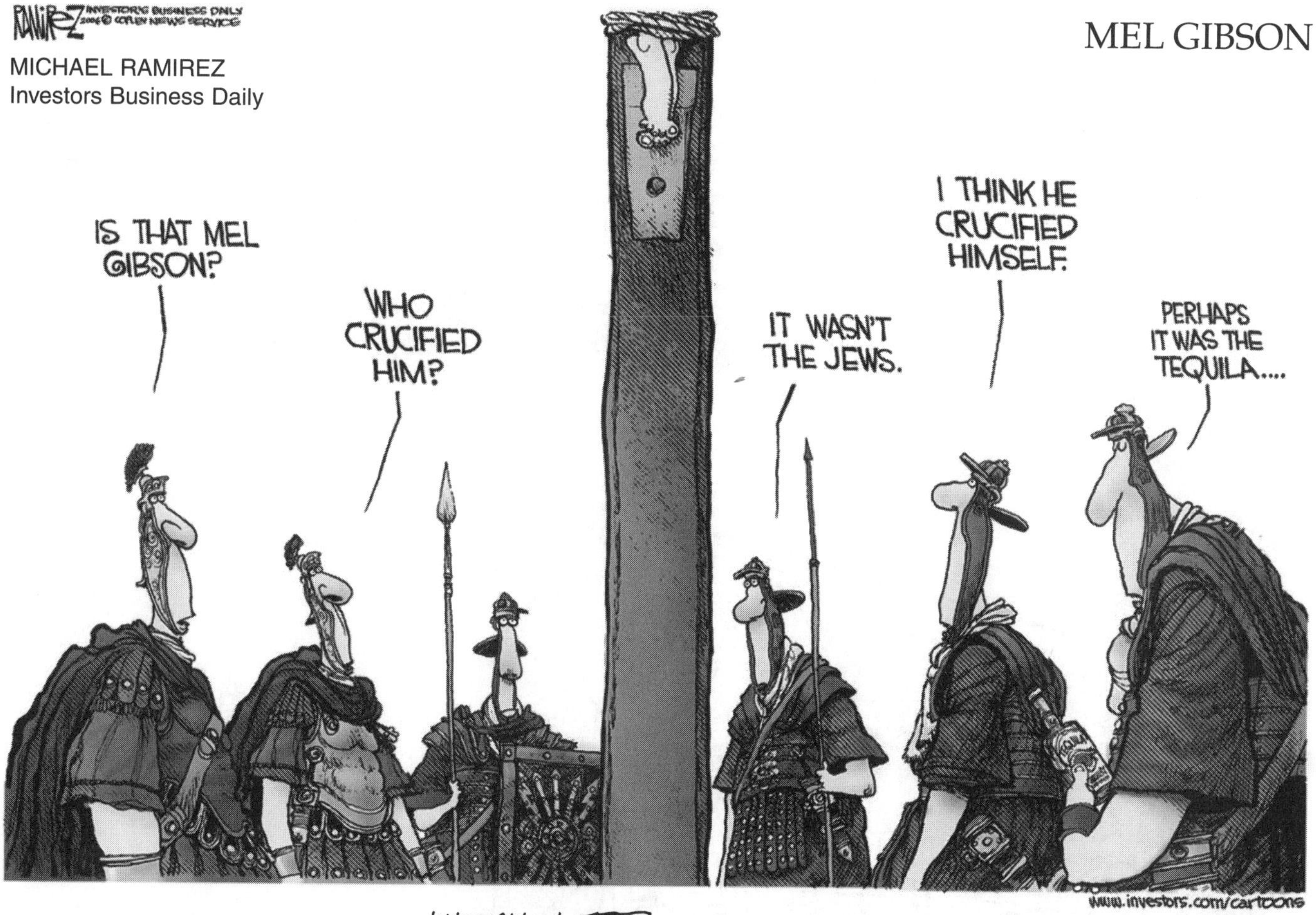
IS THAT MEL GIBSON?
WHO CRUCIFIED HIM?
IT WASN'T THE JEWS.
I THINK HE CRUCIFIED HIMSELF.
PERHAPS IT WAS THE TEQUILA....
www.investors.com/cartoons

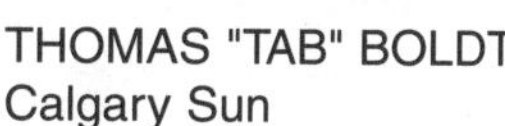

THOMAS "TAB" BOLDT
Calgary Sun

tabtoons@telus.net
caglecartoons.com
MEL GIBSON INCOMING..
ISRAEL
THE NEWEST HEZBOLLAH ROCKET..

JOHN DEERING
Arkansas Democrat Gazette

DEERING
LETHAL WEAPON V
LISTEN, MEL, ABOUT YOUR LATEST SEQUEL...

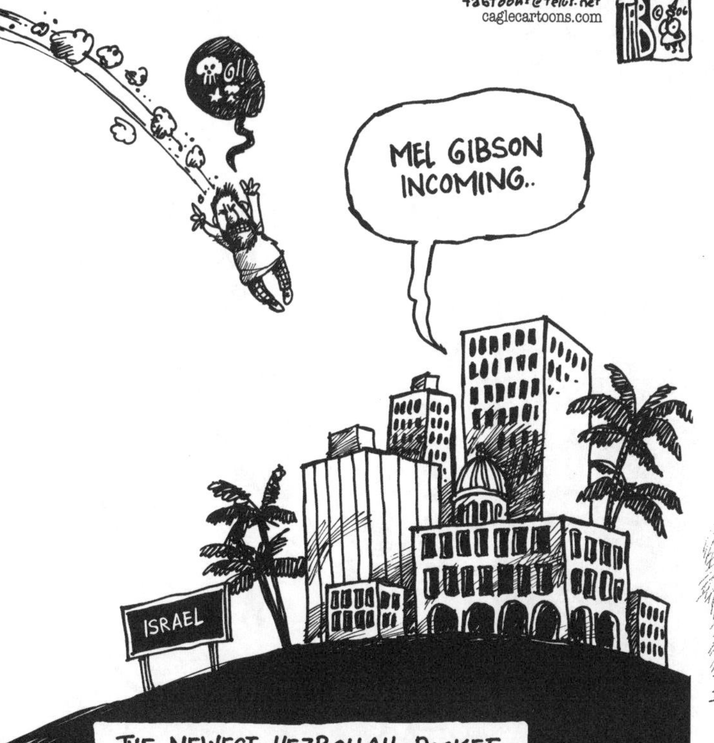

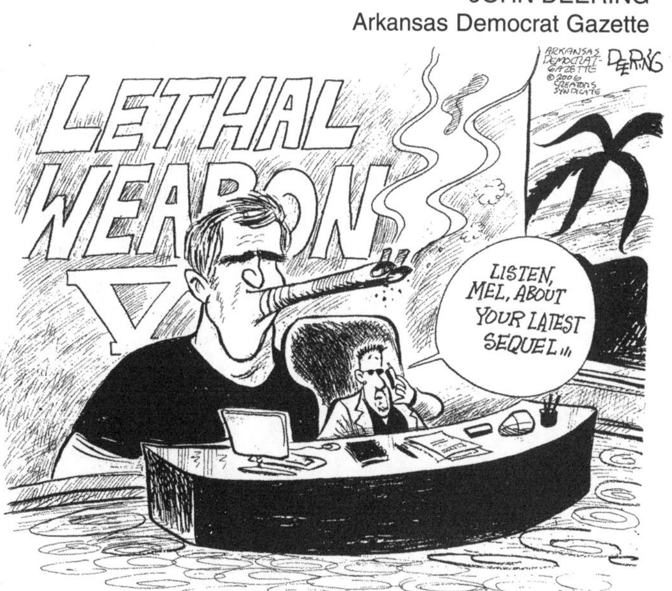

MATT DAVIES
Journal News (NY)

CLAY JONES
Freelance-Star (VA)

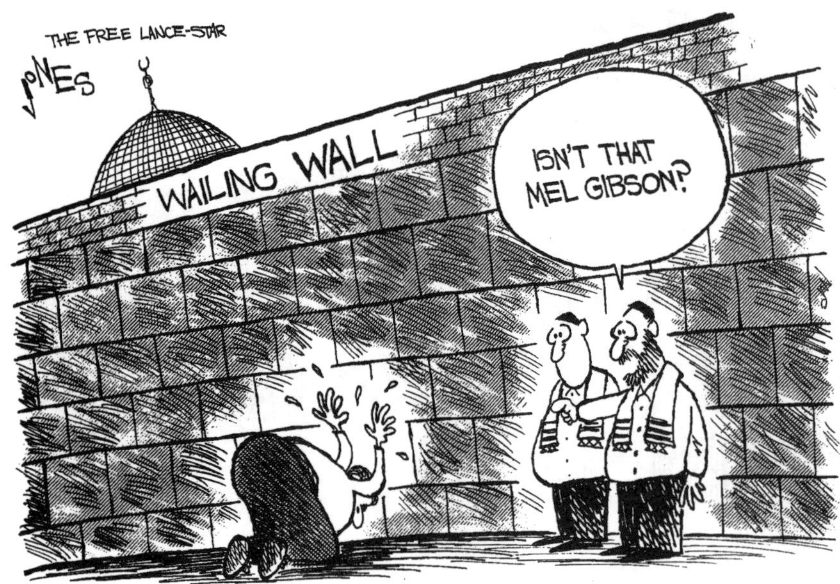

STEVE GREENBERG
Ventura County Star

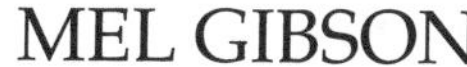

MEL GIBSON

The U.N. considers Israel's point of view...
MEL
MEL
MEL
HUFFAKER www.CAGLECARTOONS.COM

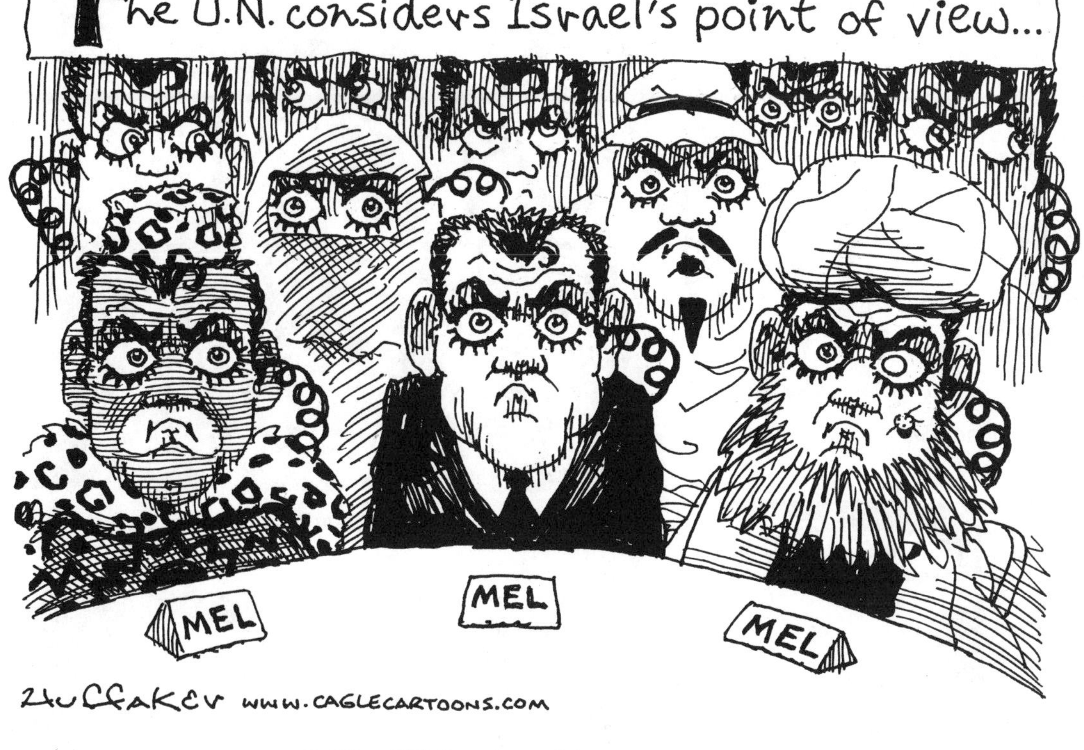

SANDY HUFFAKER
Cagle Cartoons

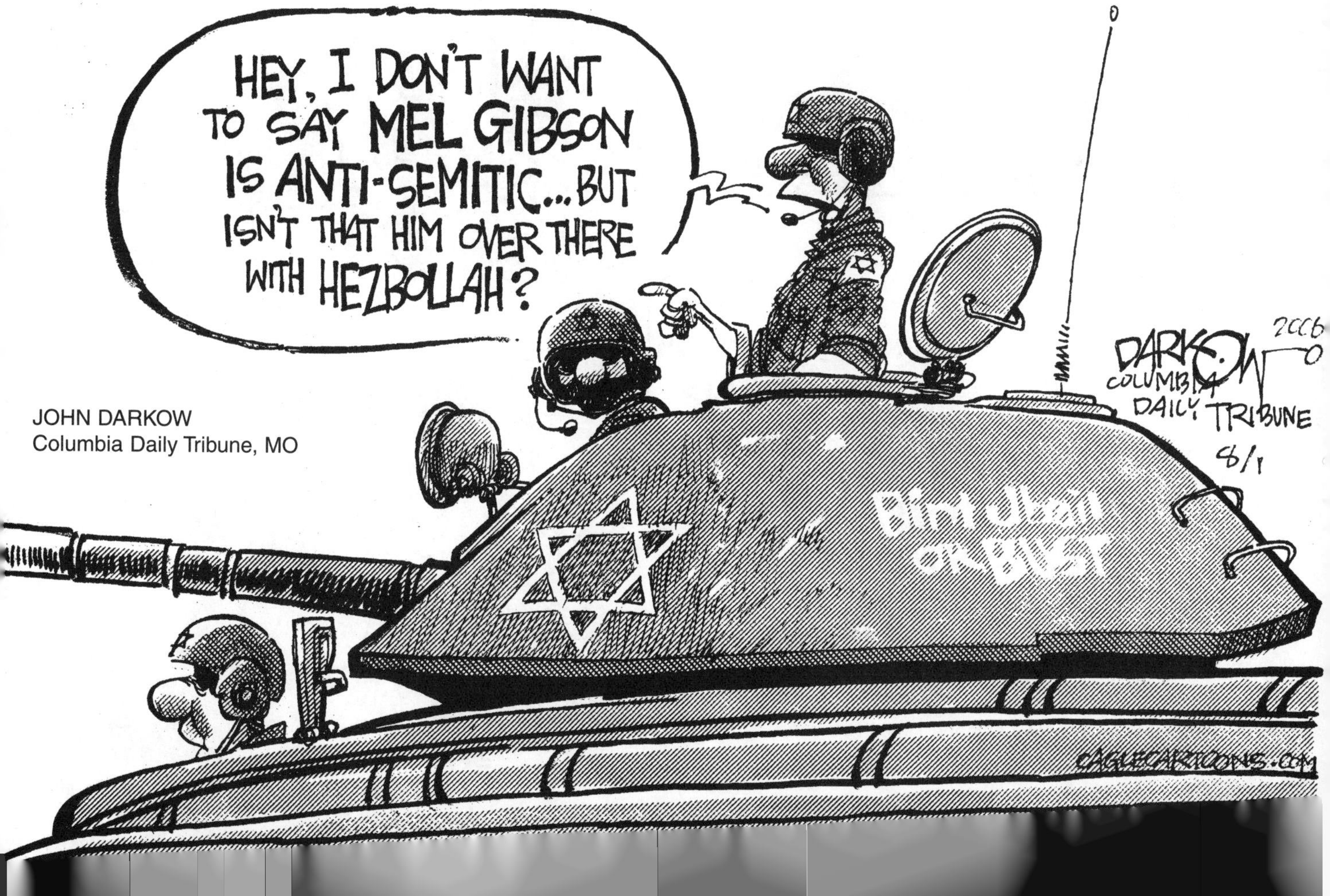
HEY, I DON'T WANT TO SAY MEL GIBSON IS ANTI-SEMITIC... BUT ISN'T THAT HIM OVER THERE WITH HEZBOLLAH?
Bint Jbail OR BUST
DARKOW 2006 COLUMBIA DAILY TRIBUNE 8/1
CAGLECARTOONS.COM

JOHN DARKOW
Columbia Daily Tribune, MO

MIKE LESTER, Rome News-Tribune (GA)

STEVE SACK, Minneapolis Star-Tribune

INGRID RICE, British Columbia, Canada

WALT HANDELSMAN, Newsday

STEVE KELLEY, New Orleans Times Picayune

DANA SUMMERS, Orlando Sentinel

MICHAEL DEADDER
Halifax Daily News

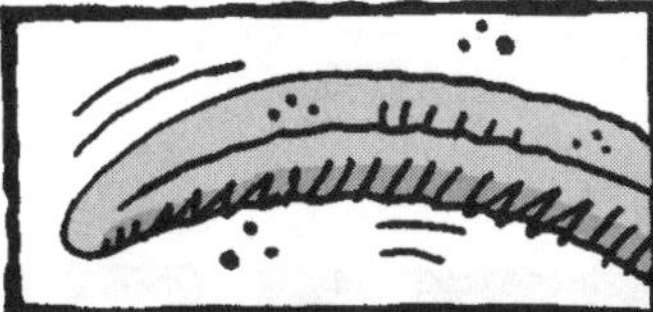

DAVID FITZSIMMONS
Arizona Daily Star

BRUCE PLANTE
Chattanooga
Times Free Press

JEFF KOTERBA, Omaha World Herald

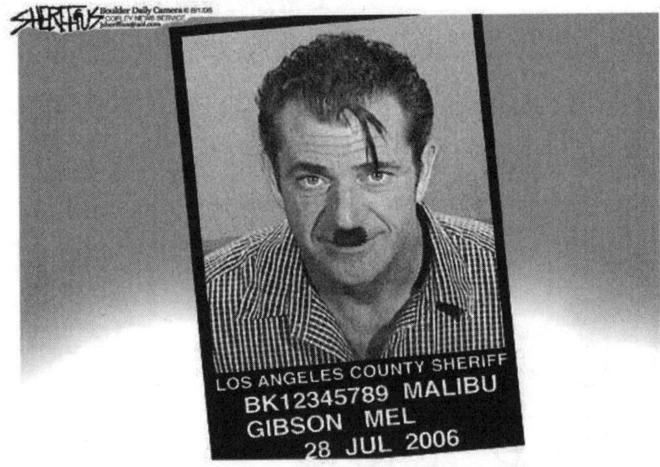

JOHN SHERFFIUS, Boulder Daily Camera

KEVIN SIERS, Charlotte Observer

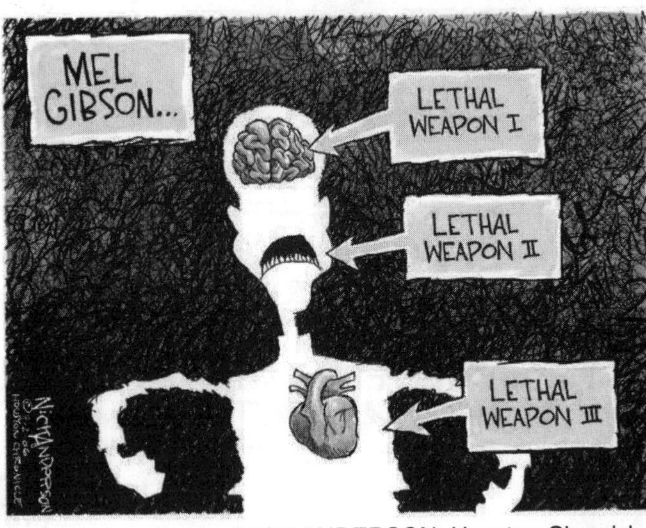

NICK ANDERSON, Houston Chronicle

MEL GIBSON

DARYL CAGLE
MSNBC.com

STEVE BENSON
Arizona Republic

Cheney Shoots

While out hunting quail on a southern Texas ranch, Vice President Dick Cheney accidentally shot his 78-year-old attorney friend Harry Whittington. The White House did not disclose information on the shooting to the public until more than a day later, at which time the Cheney camp insisted that Whittington was not really shot, but "peppered" with birdshot pellets in the face, neck, and torso. Cartoonists were clearly relieved by this news.

DON WRIGHT
Palm Beach Post

HENRY PAYNE, Detroit News

MIKE LESTER
Rome News-Tribune (GA)

CAL GRONDAHL, Utah Standard Examiner

V.P.

GRONDAHL
STANDARD EXAMINER

"You just shot a rich lawyer. This will only increase your popularity in the polls."

JIMMY MARGULIES, The Record (NJ)

HE'S A POINTER

RANDY BISH, Pittsburgh Tribune-Review

BOB ENGLEHART, Hartford Courant

CHUCK ASAY, Colorado Springs Gazette

BILL DAY, Memphis Commercial Appeal

MIKE KEEFE, Denver Post

DICK LOCHER, Chicago Tribune

PAT BAGLEY, Salt Lake Tribune, UT

GARY VARVEL, Indianapolis Star

JIMMY MARGULIES
The Record (NJ)

JACK OHMAN
Portland Oregonian

DICK LOCHER, Chicago Tribune

THOMAS "TAB" BOLDT
Calgary Sun

CHENEY SHOOTS

PAUL CONRAD
Tribune Media Services

MICHAEL RAMIREZ, Investors Business Daily

JACK OHMAN, Portland Oregonian

CAMERON CARDOW, Ottawa Citizen

DREW SHENEMAN, Newark Star-Ledger

DOUG MARLETTE, Tulsa World

BILL DAY, Memphis Commercial Appeal

BOB GORRELL

DARYL CAGLE, MSNBC.com

MONTE WOLVERTON
Cagle Cartoons

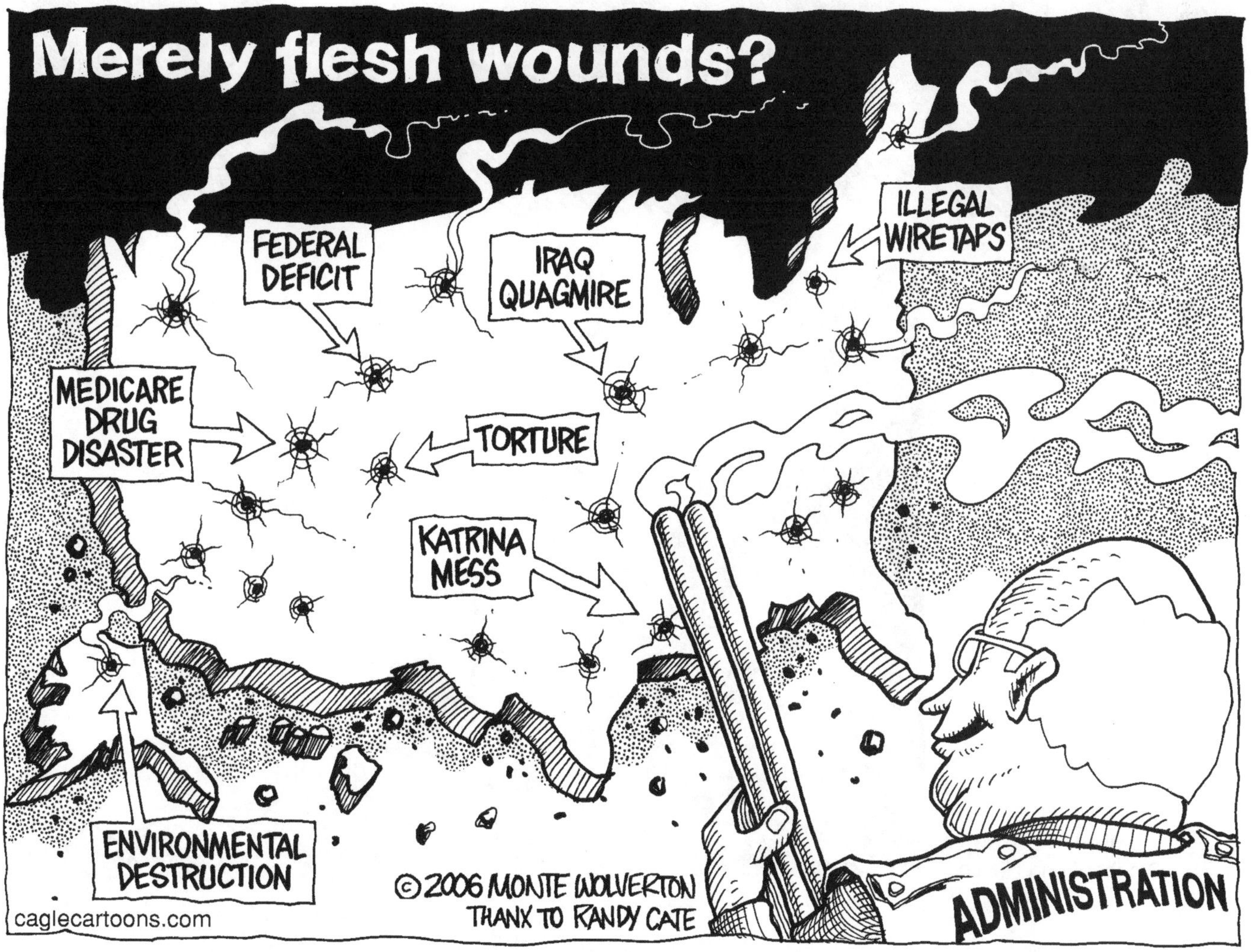

Merely flesh wounds?

ILLEGAL WIRETAPS

FEDERAL DEFICIT

IRAQ QUAGMIRE

MEDICARE DRUG DISASTER

TORTURE

KATRINA MESS

ENVIRONMENTAL DESTRUCTION

© 2006 MONTE WOLVERTON
THANX TO RANDY CATE

ADMINISTRATION

caglecartoons.com

JOHN DARKOW, Columbia Daily Tribune, MO

JEFF KOTERBA
Omaha World Herald

"STRANGEST THING, OSAMA...THEY'RE INVITATIONS TO JOIN DICK CHENEY ON HIS NEXT HUNTING TRIP."

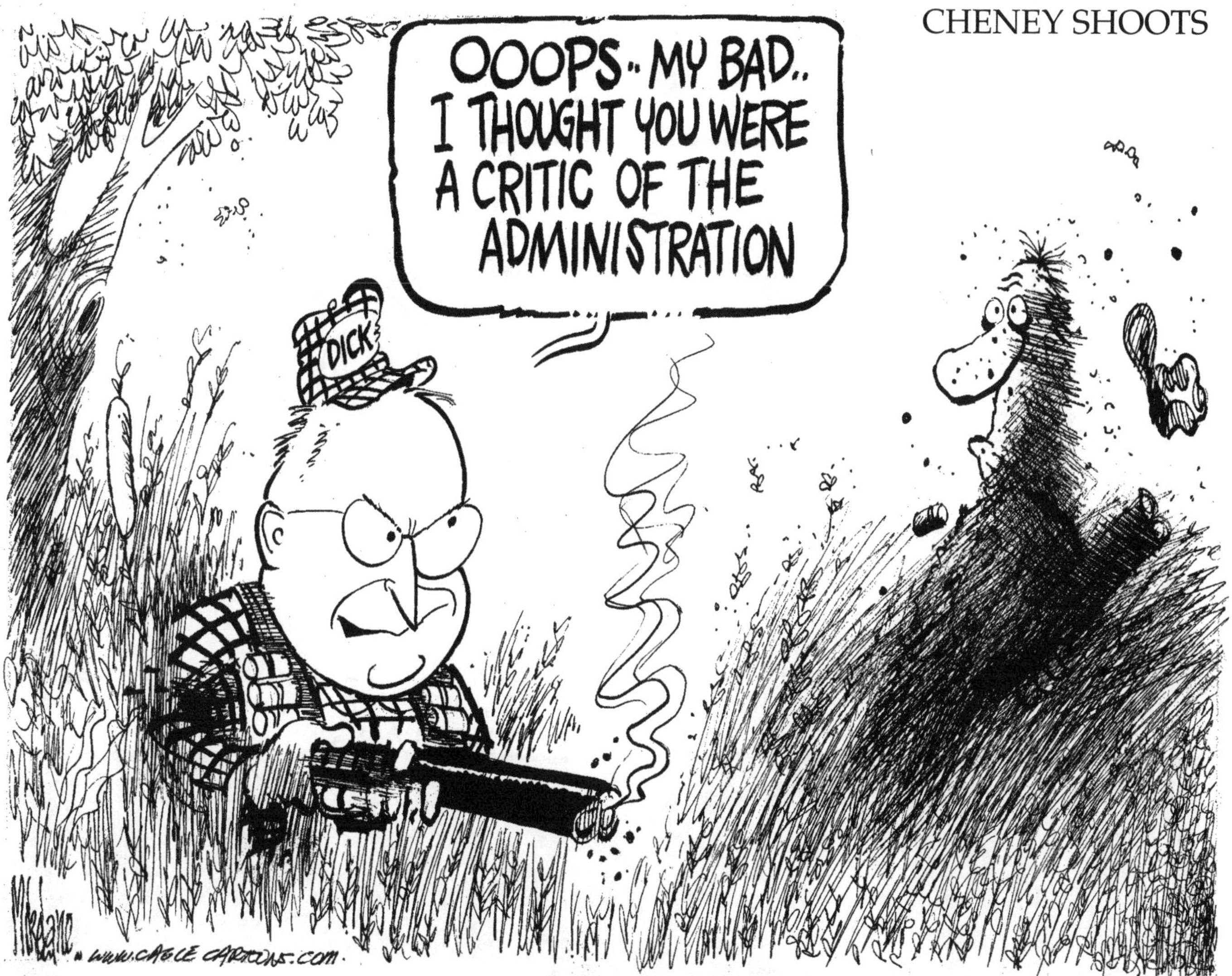

OOOPS.. MY BAD..
I THOUGHT YOU WERE
A CRITIC OF THE
ADMINISTRATION

DICK

MLane www.cagle cartoons.com

MIKE LANE, Cagle Cartoons

JOHN SHERFFIUS
Boulder Daily Camera

"And it was, I'd have to say, one of the worst days of my life..."
— Vice President Cheney

REX BABIN
Sacramento Bee

DANA SUMMERS
Orlando Sentinel

DWAYNE BOOTH
Mr. Fish

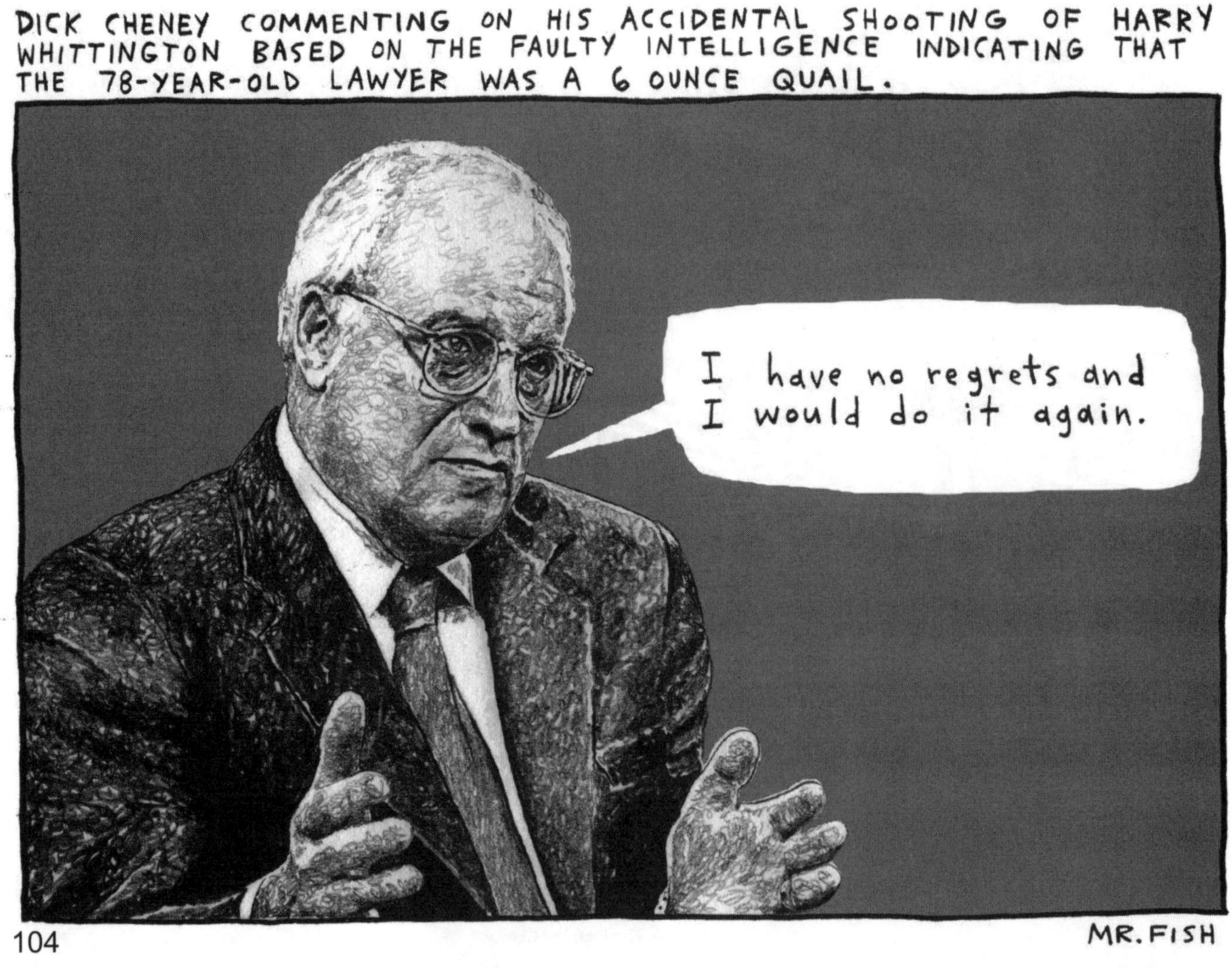

DICK CHENEY COMMENTING ON HIS ACCIDENTAL SHOOTING OF HARRY WHITTINGTON BASED ON THE FAULTY INTELLIGENCE INDICATING THAT THE 78-YEAR-OLD LAWYER WAS A 6 OUNCE QUAIL.

I have no regrets and I would do it again.

MR. FISH

REX BABIN
Sacramento Bee

ROBERT ARIAIL
The State (SC)

MIKE LANE, Cagle Cartoons

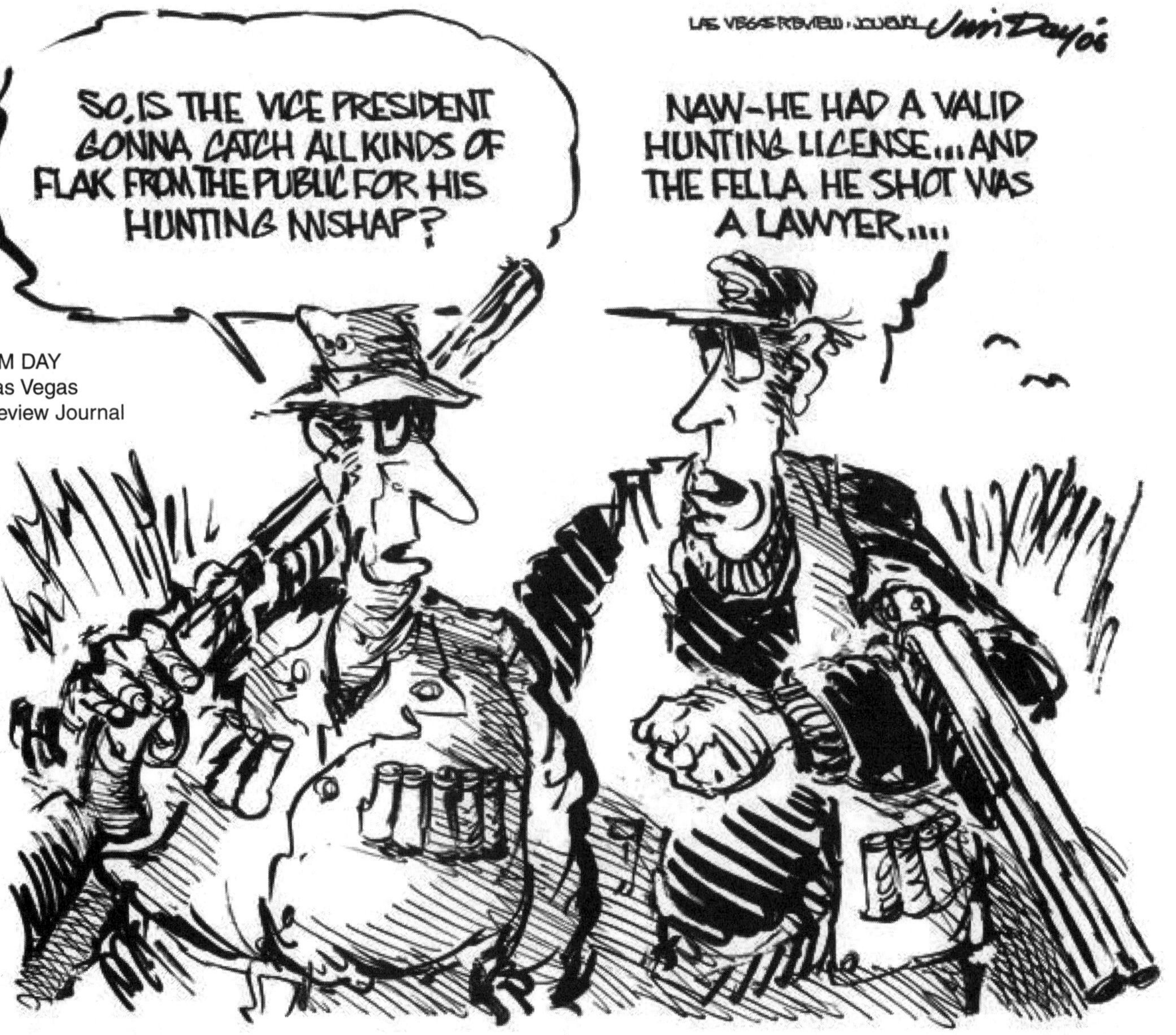

LAS VEGAS REVIEW-JOURNAL Jim Day '06

SO, IS THE VICE PRESIDENT GONNA CATCH ALL KINDS OF FLAK FROM THE PUBLIC FOR HIS HUNTING MISHAP?

NAW—HE HAD A VALID HUNTING LICENSE... AND THE FELLA HE SHOT WAS A LAWYER....

JIM DAY
Las Vegas
Review Journal

STEVE BENSON, Arizona Republic

ED STEIN, Rocky Mountain News

JEN SORENSEN
Slowpoke

SLOWPOKE

THE WEEK AFTER CHENEY'S HUNTING ACCIDENT, TIME MAGAZINE RAN A COVER STORY ABOUT HIS **RESOLUTENESS** TO DO THINGS HIS WAY.

TIME

STICKING TO HIS GUNS

STICKING TO HIS GUNS! **WOO!**

W THE PRESIDENT

GIVEN THIS TENDENCY TOWARDS SPIN-AFFIRMING EUPHEMISMS, WHAT COVERS CAN WE EXPECT TO SEE IN THE FUTURE?

BRUCE PLANTE
Chattanooga
Times Free Press

Deadly Spinach

Spinach is supposed to be good for you, but this year it took a turn for the dangerous. Thousands of bags of the leafy greens were recalled when one person died and more than a hundred became ill after eating spinach tainted with E. coli bacteria. Many cartoonists turned to classic spinach-champion Popeye for ironic inspiration.

"Oh, one last thing . . . got any bagged spinach in your carry-on?"

BRUCE BEATTIE, Daytona News-Journal

GARY VARVEL, Indianapolis Star

SHERFFIUS Boulder Daily Camera © 9/18/06 COPLEY NEWS SERVICE jsherffius@aol.com

JOHN SHERFFIUS
Boulder Daily Camera

SPINACH

CHRISTO KOMARNITSKI
Bulgaria

DON WRIGHT, Palm Beach Post

CAMERON CARDOW
Ottawa Citizen

JOE HELLER
Green Bay
Press-Gazette

THIS GREEN STUFF IS MAKING SOME SICK AND IT'S SUPPOSED TO MAKE YOU STRONG.

BAGGED SPINACH

JoeHeller ©2006 GREENBAY PRESS-GAZETTE

THOMAS "TAB" BOLDT
Calgary Sun

JIMMY MARGULIES, The Record (NJ)

DREW SHENEMAN, Newark Star-Ledger

STEVE BENSON, Arizona Republic

REX BABIN
Sacramento Bee

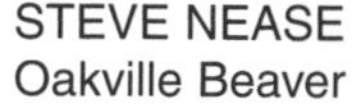
STEVE NEASE
Oakville Beaver

MONTE WOLVERTON
Cagle Cartoons

R.P. OVERMYER, Hollywood Dog

Hamas Wins

This terrorist group Hamas won a majority in the Palestinian parliament in democratic elections in early 2006, defeating the long ruling Fatah party of Palestinian president Mahmoud Abbas. Hamas and Fatah fought continuously and Western countries stopped propping up the dysfunctional state by withholding aid payments. As chaos spread, Israel invaded the Gaza Strip in response to the kidnapping of an Israeli soldier.

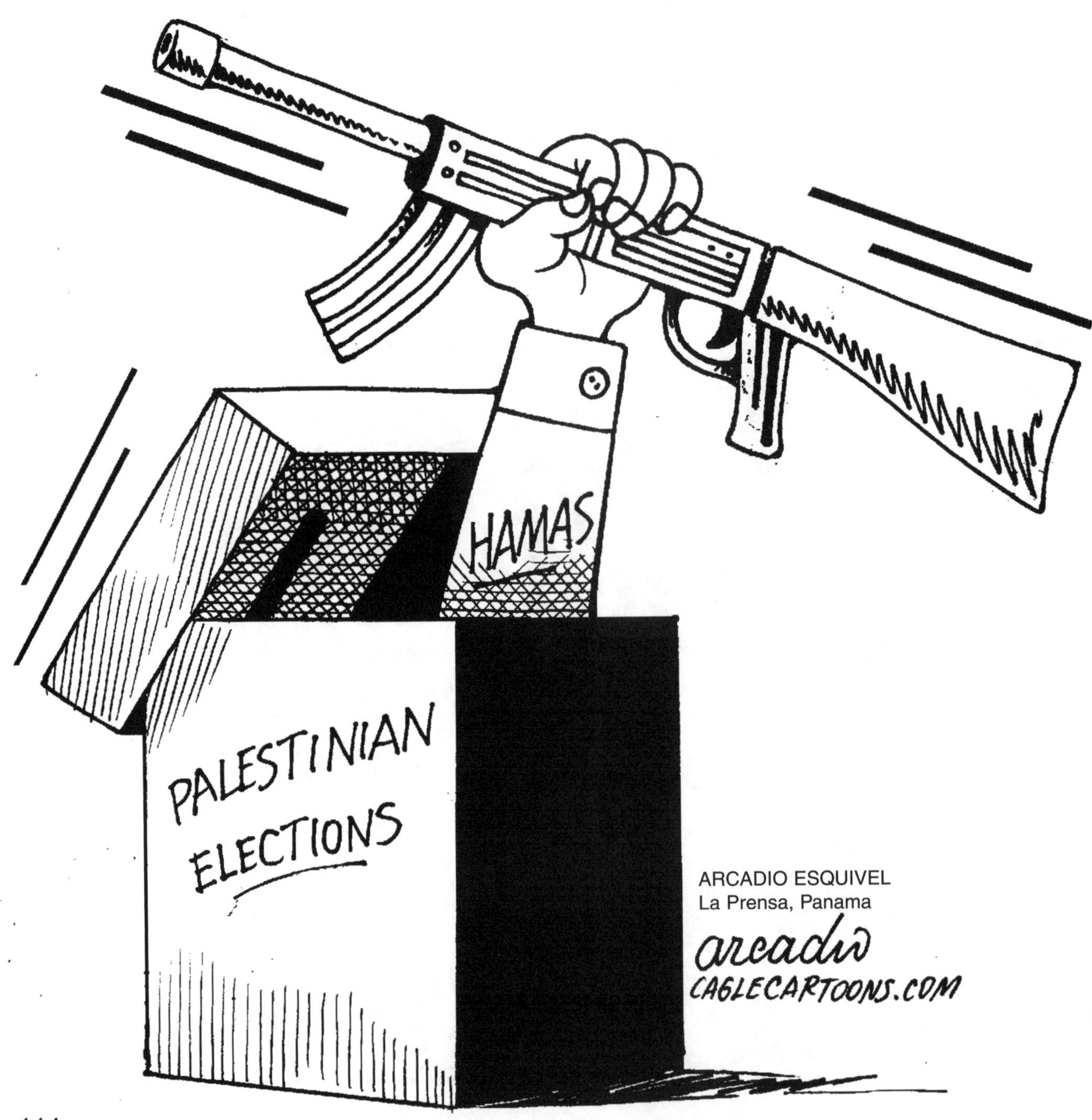

ARCADIO ESQUIVEL
La Prensa, Panama

JIM DAY
Las Vegas Review-Journal

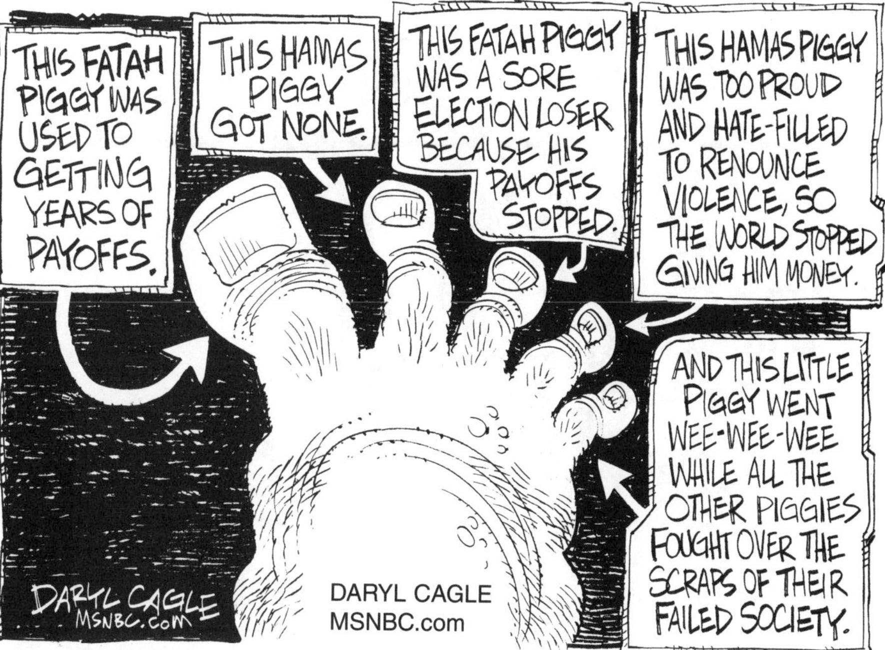

DARYL CAGLE
MSNBC.com

STEVE SACK
Minneapolis Star Tribune

DAN WASSERMAN
Boston Globe

LARRY WRIGHT
Detroit News

CHRIS BRITT
State Journal-Register (IL)

DON WRIGHT
Palm Beach Post

PAUL CONRAD

BILL DAY, Memphis Commercial Appeal

RICHARD CROWSON, Witchita Eagle

DARYL CAGLE, MSNBC.com

"A Palestinian future blew itself up in a crowded polling place..."

JIMMY MARGULIES, The Record

JOHN BRANCH, San Antonio Express-News

CHIP BOK, Akron Beacon-Journal

THOMAS "TAB" BOLDT, Calgary Sun

ROBERT ARIAIL, The State (SC)

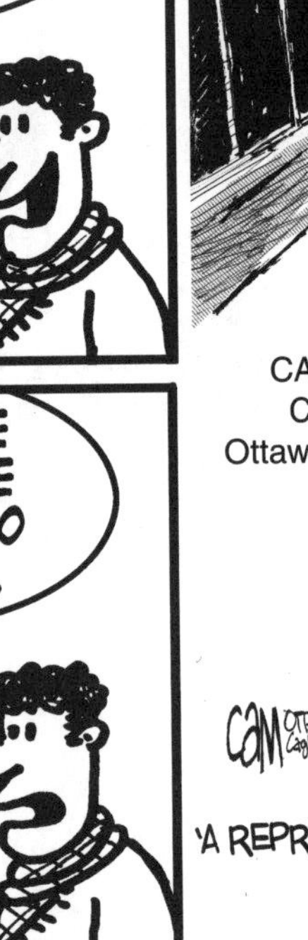

YAAKOV KIRSCHEN, Dry Bones, Jerusalem Post, Israel

CAMERON CARDOW
Ottawa Citizen
Canada

'A REPRESENTATIVE FROM THE NEW PALESTINIAN GOVERNMENT TO SEE YOU, MR. PRESIDENT'

SANDY HUFFAKER

STEVE GREENBERG, Ventura County Star

PATRICK CHAPPATTE, International Herald Tribune

DICK LOCHER, Chicago Tribune

RAINER HACHFELD, Germany

JEFF KOTERBA, Omaha World Herald

Buffett's Billions

The second-richest man on earth, Warren Buffett, made the largest charitable gift in history to a foundation run by the richest man on earth, Bill Gates. Buffett will give away about $37 billion to five foundations in annual donations of Berkshire Hathaway stock, with the largest chunk going to the Bill and Melinda Gates Foundation. Buffet's generosity impressed just about everyone, including editorial cartoonists—and that's saying a lot.

DAVID HORSEY
Seattle Post Intelligencer

"MUMMY! DADDY'S NOT GOING TO GIVE AWAY MY *INHERITANCE* TO THE *GATES FOUNDATION*, IS HE?!"

BRUCE PLANTE
Chattanooga Times Free Press

MIKE LANE
Cagle Cartoons

JIMMY MARGULIES
The Record (NJ)

JOE HELLER
Green Bay Press Gazette

DARYL CAGLE
MSNBC.com

WAIT, YOU'RE SAYING GREED IS **NOT** GOOD?

BUFFETT

Englehart ©6/28/06 HARTFORD COURANT

caglecartoons.com

courant.com/boblog

BOB ENGLEHART, Hartford Courant

ROBERT ARIAIL
The State (SC)

PATRICK CHAPPATTE, International Herald Tribune

BUY!

SELL!

GIVE AWAY!!

THE WARREN BUFFETT EFFECT

CHAPPATTE
Int'l Herald Tribune

MATT DAVIES
Journal News (NY)

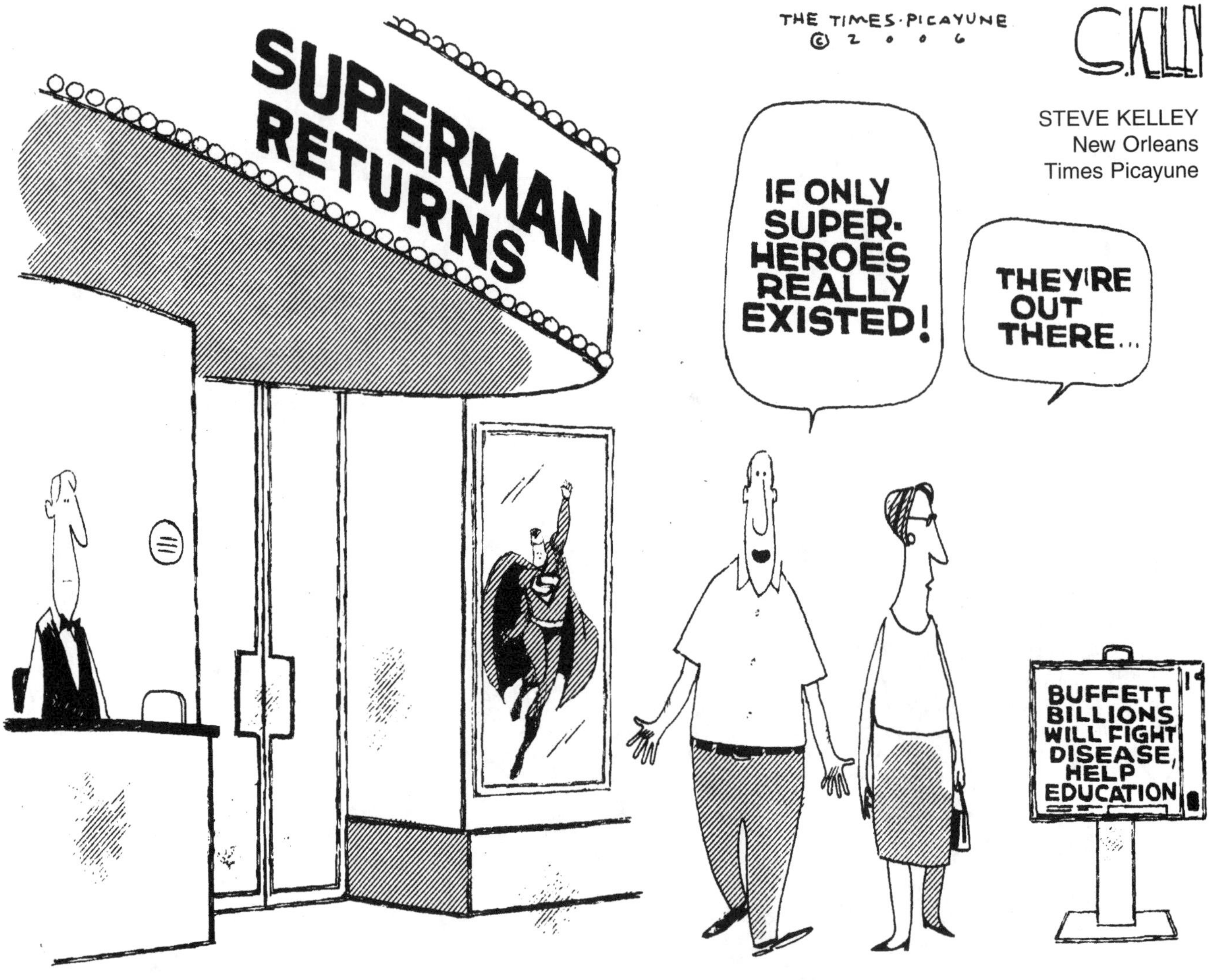

THE TIMES-PICAYUNE © 2006
S.KELLEY

SUPERMAN RETURNS

IF ONLY SUPER-HEROES REALLY EXISTED!

THEY'RE OUT THERE...

BUFFETT BILLIONS WILL FIGHT DISEASE, HELP EDUCATION

STEVE KELLEY
New Orleans
Times Picayune

HENRY PAYNE, Detroit News

Phone
FUNDED BY A GRANT FROM THE GATES FOUNDATION.
H. Payne
EMAIL: hpayne@detnews.com ©06

JEFF STAHLER
Columbus Dispatch

STAHLER. 2006.
DO YOU HAVE ANY PHILANTHROPIC POWERS?

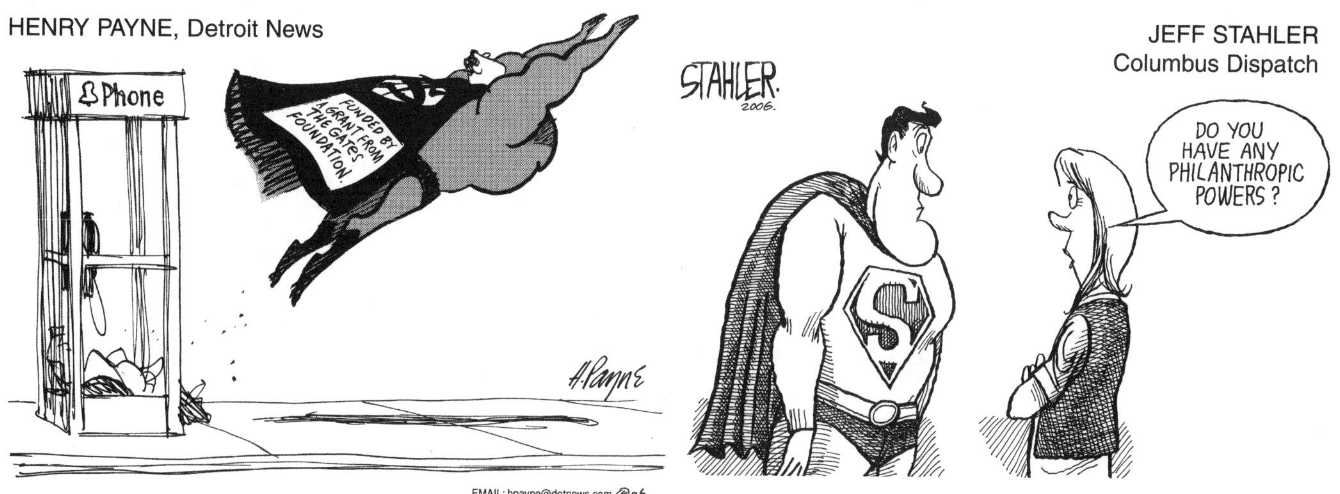

R.J. MATSON, St. Louis Post Dispatch

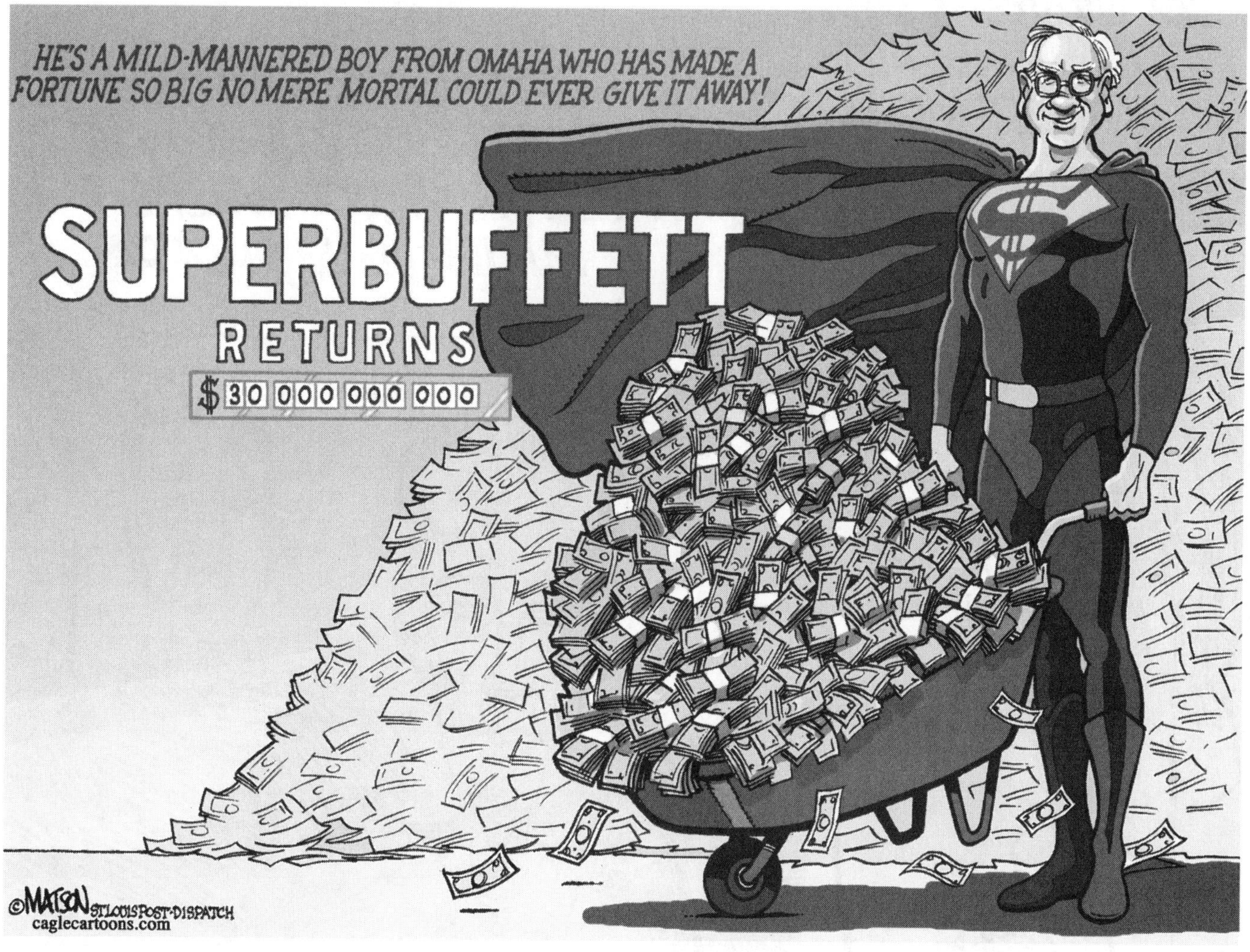
HE'S A MILD-MANNERED BOY FROM OMAHA WHO HAS MADE A FORTUNE SO BIG NO MERE MORTAL COULD EVER GIVE IT AWAY!
SUPERBUFFETT
RETURNS
$30 000 000 000
©MATSON ST. LOUIS POST-DISPATCH
caglecartoons.com

John Mark Karr

He first burst on the scene with his confession to the murder of child beauty queen, JonBenet Ramsey. The John Mark Karr story made great cartoon fodder: an American school teacher and connoisseur of child pornography confessing to a decade-old, high-profile murder. He was arrested in Thailand and drank champagne on a well-publicized first-class flight to the USA. Journalists, cartoonists and much of the public jumped on the story, assuming that Karr really was the killer, but he turned out only to be a nut. Karr wasn't even prosecuted for child pornography charges, as prosecutors in California misplaced the evidence in his case.

J.D. CROWE
Mobile Register

GUY BADEAUX, Journal LeDroit

JOE HELLER, Green Bay Press-Gazette

WHO WOULD DO SOMETHING LIKE THAT?
WHAT? FALSELY CONFESS?
-KILL HER?
-OR, DRESS A LITTLE GIRL LIKE PEDOPHILE BAIT?
NEWS
JOHN MARK KARR CHARGES DROPPED: JONBENET KILLER STILL UNKNOWN
©MIKE LESTER Rome News Tribune www.cagecartoons.com

MIKE LESTER
Rome News Tribune (GA)

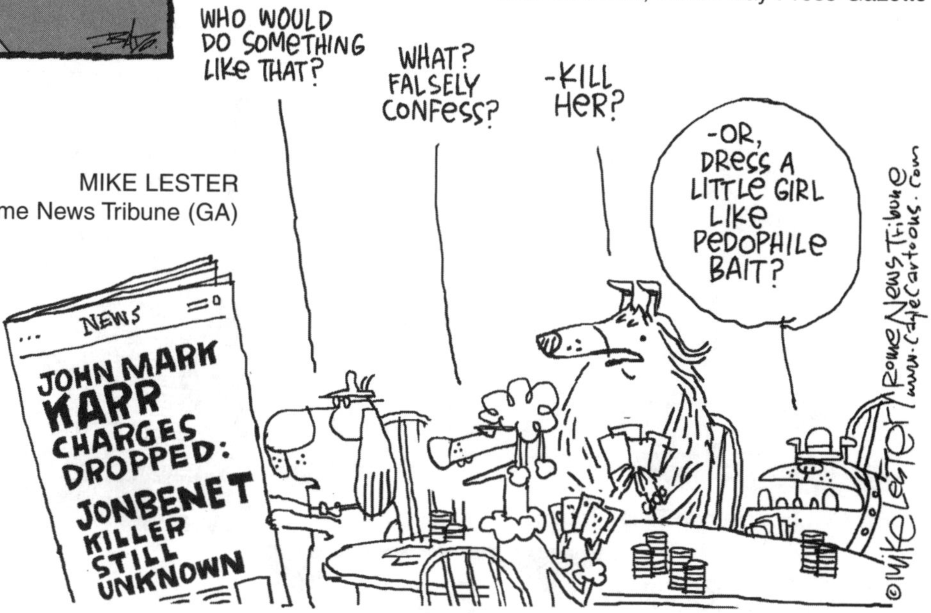

DARYL CAGLE
MSNBC.com

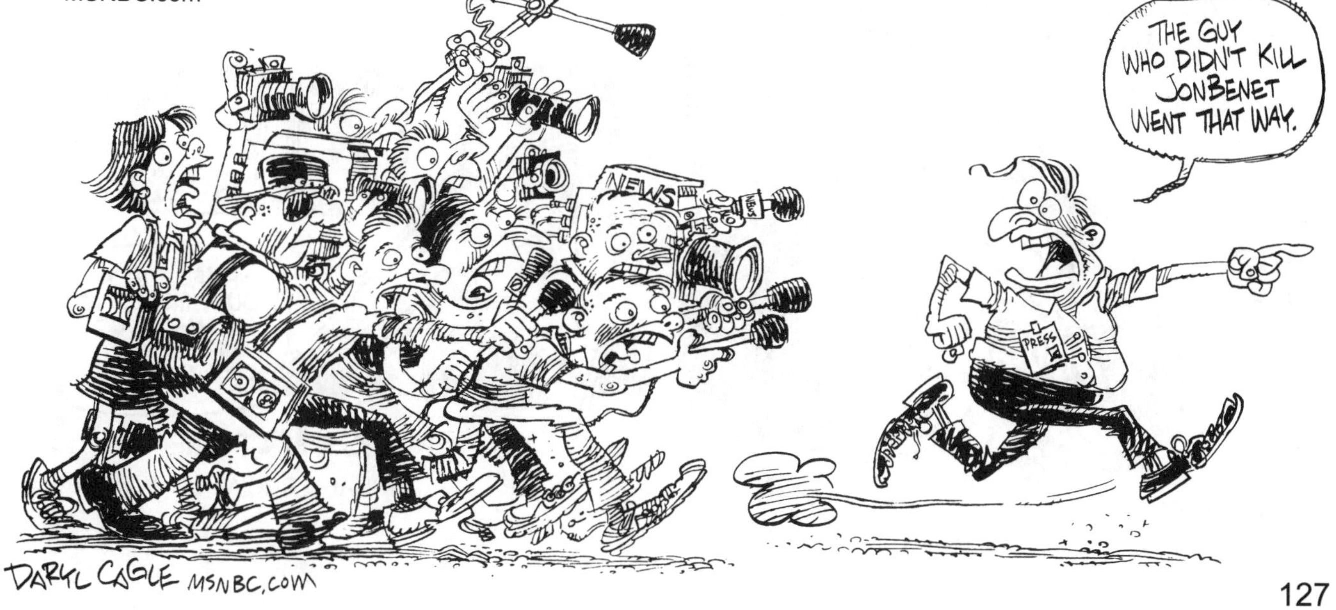

THE GUY WHO DIDN'T KILL JONBENET WENT THAT WAY.
NEWS
PRESS
DARYL CAGLE MSNBC.COM

CAMERON CARDOW, Ottawa Citizen (Canada)

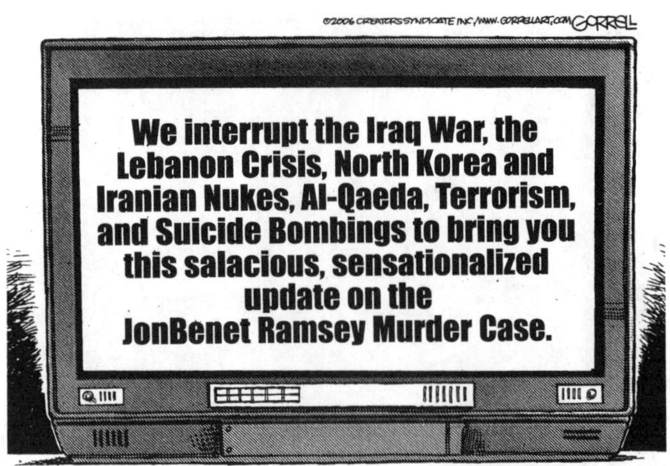

BOB GORRELL

JOHN COLE, Scranton Times Tribune

CLAY JONES, Freelance-Star (VA)

STEVE NEASE, Oakville Beaver (Canada)

RICHARD CROWSON, Witchita Eagle

JOHN MARK KARR

ED STEIN
Rocky Mountain News

MIKE THOMPSON
Detroit Free-Press

YOU WANT THE MEDIA TO SHOW AN INTEREST IN THE CASE, DON'T YOU?

BLOND hair dye

LICE LINE DO NOT

DO NOT

Arab Port Deal

Controversy erupted this year when the Bush administration approved the sale of six major U.S. seaport operations to a United Arab Emirates company. Several politicians said the takeover would compromise the nation's security, while Bush argued that delaying the deal would send the wrong message to U.S. allies. Cartoonists love controversies, and they had a field day with this one.

THOMAS "TAB" BOLDT
Calgary Sun

PORT SAFETY

THE SALT LAKE TRIBUNE BAGLEY '06

PAT BAGLEY
Salt Lake
Tribune (UT)

MIKE LANE
Cagle Cartoons

MIKE KEEFE
Denver Post

CLAY JONES
Freelance-Star (VA)

CHRISTO KOMARNITSKI
Bulgaria

" I DIDN'T GET MY SUPERHUMAN POWER BY BEING SOFT ON TERRORISM!"

R.J. MATSON
St. Louis Post-Dispatch

WAYNE STAYSKAL
Tribune Media Services

DANA SUMMERS
Orlando Sentinel

ROBERT ARIAIL
The State (SC)

GARY BROOKINS
Richmond Times-Dispatch

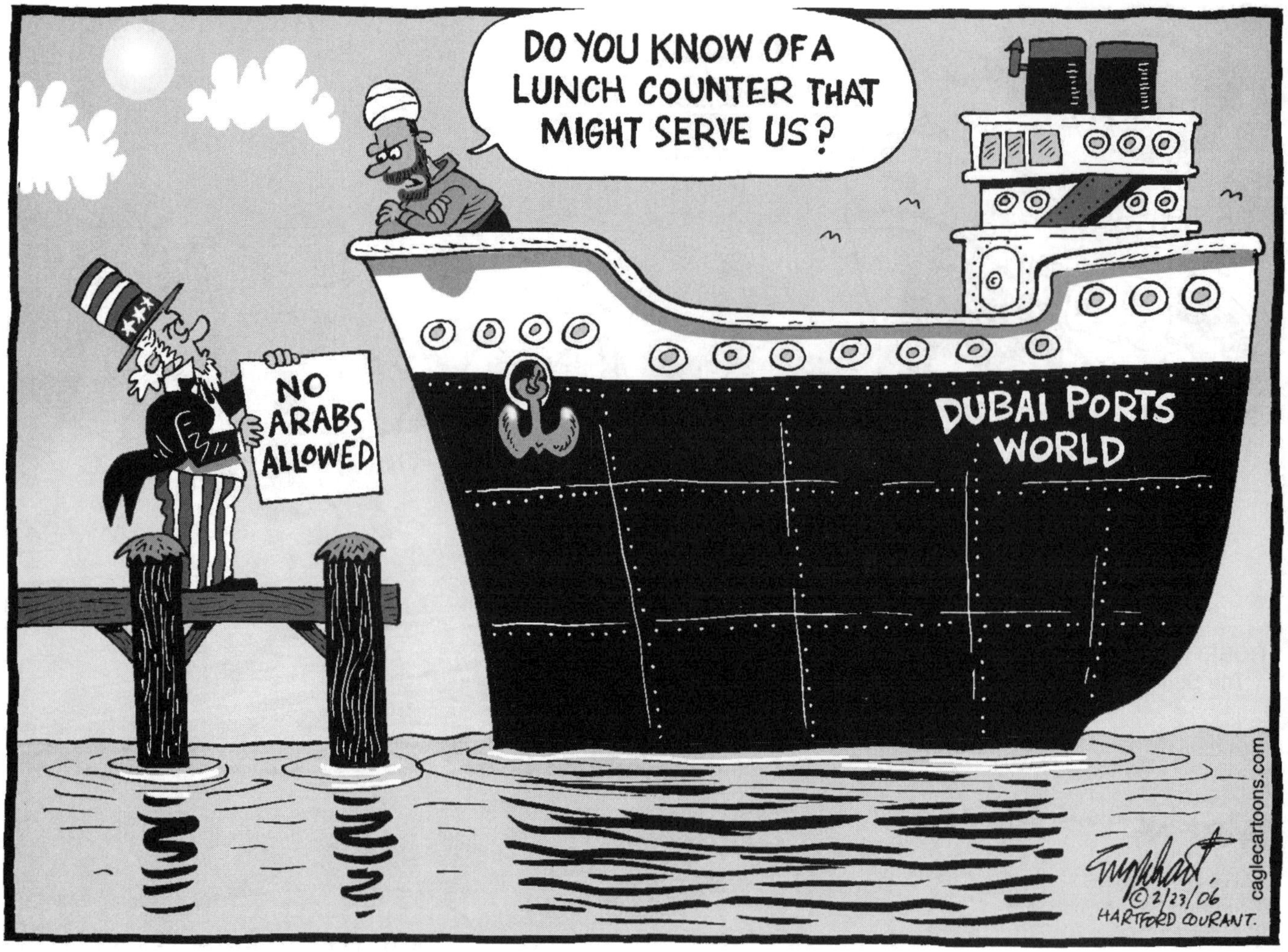
DO YOU KNOW OF A LUNCH COUNTER THAT MIGHT SERVE US?
NO ARABS ALLOWED
DUBAI PORTS WORLD
caglecartoons.com
Englehart ©2/23/06 HARTFORD COURANT.

BOB ENGLEHART, Hartford Courant

DUBAI PORTS WORLD
DARYL CAGLE MSNBC.COM

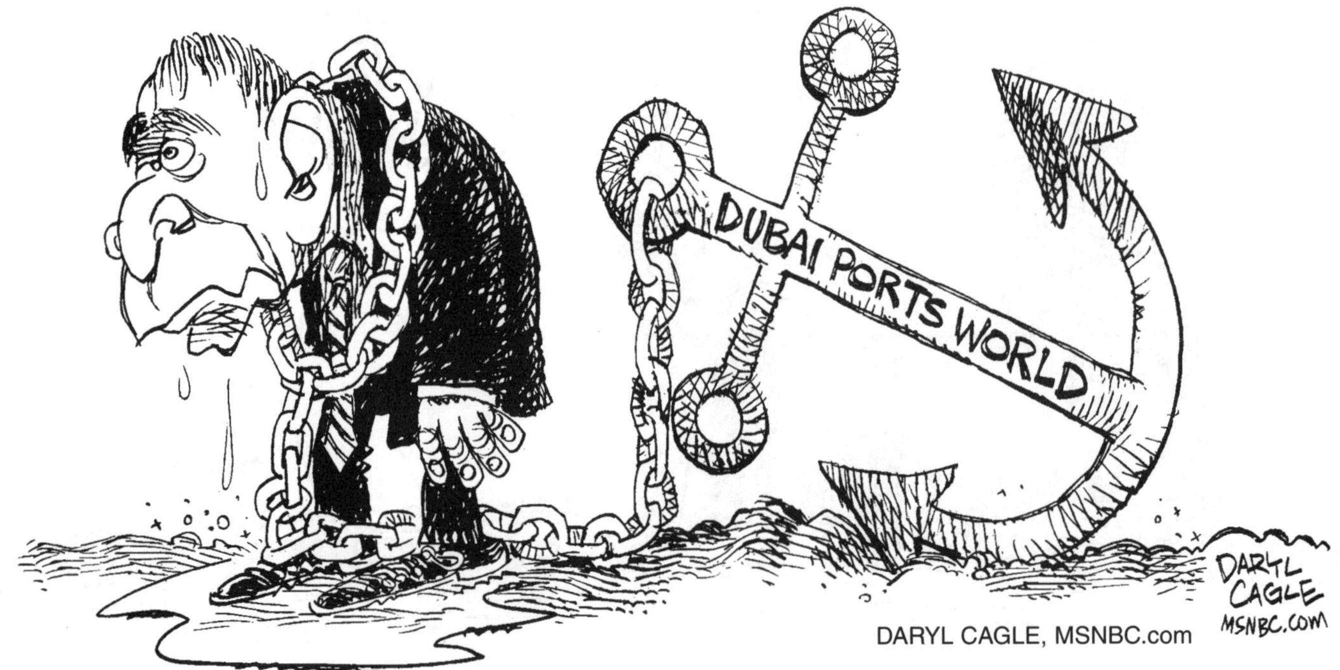

DARYL CAGLE, MSNBC.com

DARYL CAGLE
MSNBC.com

STEVE BENSON, Arizona Republic

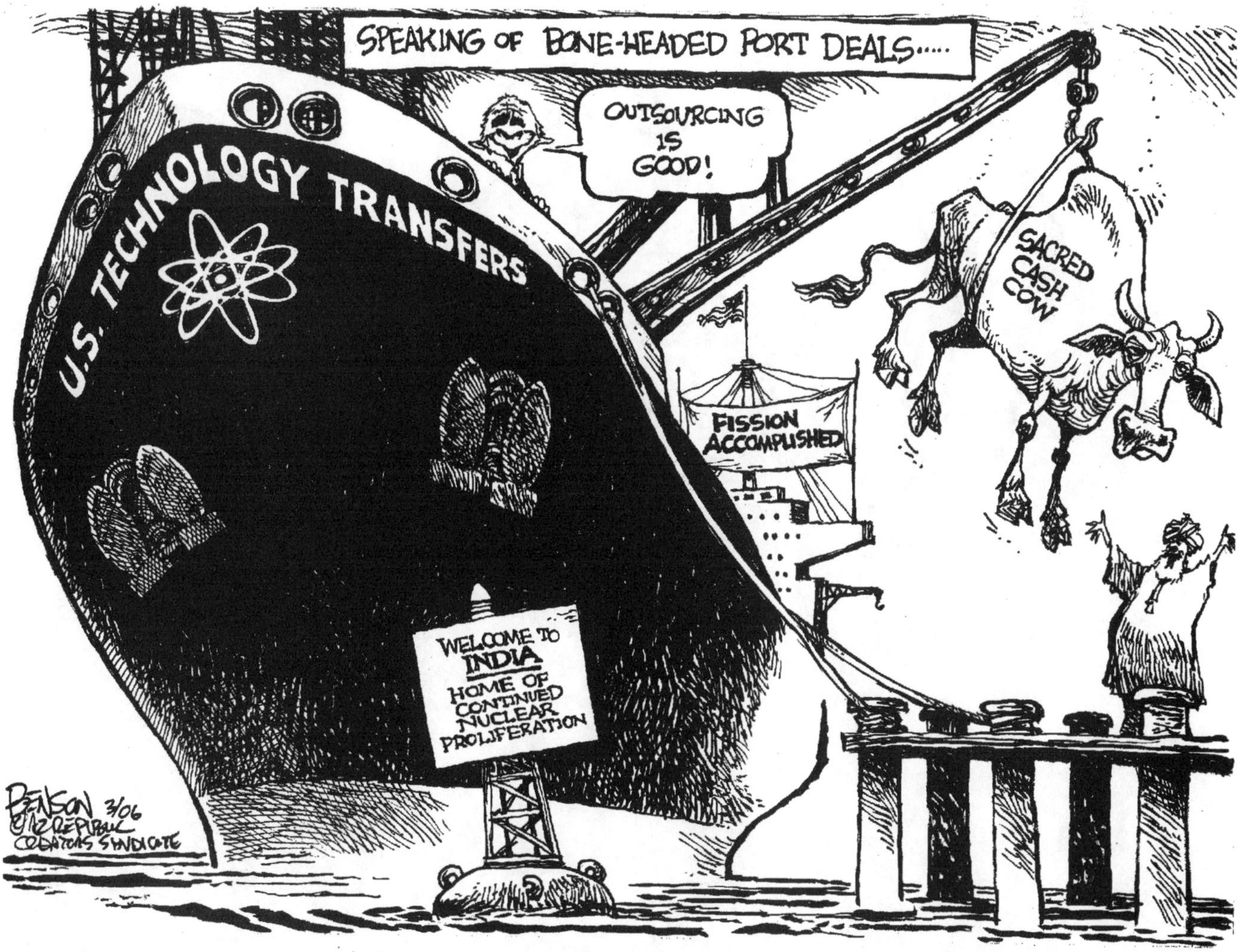

MIKE KEEFE
Denver Post

STEVE SACK
Minneapolis
Star-Tribune

ARAB PORT DEAL

HENRY PAYNE
Detroit News

"LET U.S. COMPANIES INTO OUR PORTS? AREN'T THEY THE COUNTRY THAT BRED THE OKLAHOMA CITY BOMBERS?"

PAT BAGLEY
Salt Lake Tribune (UT)

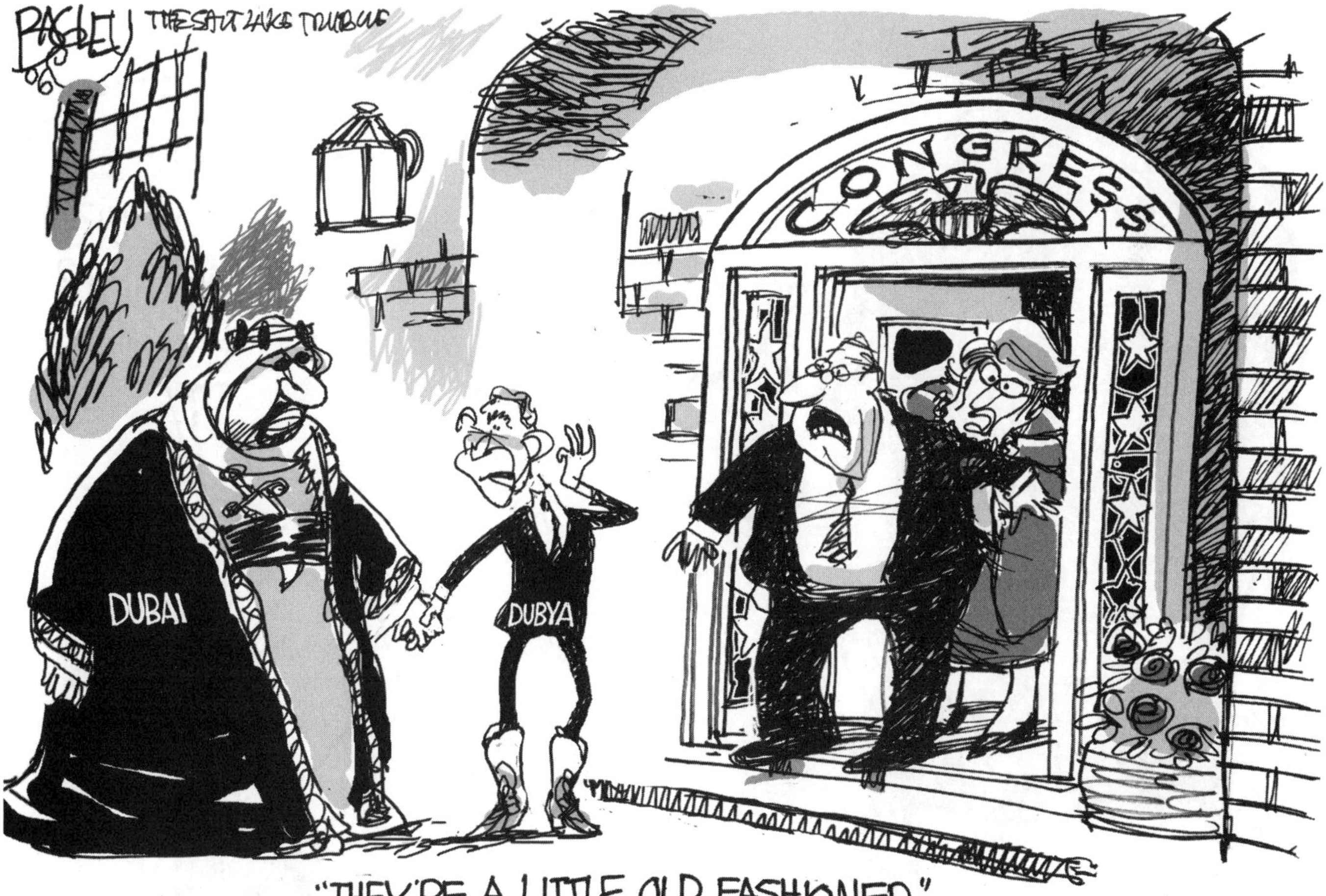

BAGLEY '06 THE SALT LAKE TRIBUNE

CONGRESS

DUBAI

DUBYA

"THEY'RE A LITTLE OLD FASHIONED."

Barry Bonds

San Francisco Giants slugger Barry Bonds surpassed Babe Ruth's home-run record this year on his reportedly steroid-aided sprint toward the all-time home-run crown. Cartoonists were quick to draw asterisks next to Bonds' name in the record books.

JEFF STAHLER
Columbus Dispatch

SYRINGE

STICK A FORK IN HIM...
I THINK HE'S DONE

MIKE LESTER
Rome News-Tribune (GA)

JOHN COLE, Scranton
Scranton Times-Tribune

R.J. MATSON, St. Louis Post Dispatch

JIMMY MARGULIES, The Record (NJ)

STEVE BREEN, San Diego Union-Tribune

JOHN DARKOW, Columbia Daily Tribune, MO

MIKE KEEFE
Denver Post

Castro's Condition

Cuban President Fidel Castro fell ill this year with an undisclosed disease. Castro appointed his brother, Raul, to the presidency while Fidel recuperated. Citizens and cartoonists alike speculated on what was troubling the longtime communist dictator and what the world might be like if he passed away.

OSMANI SIMANCA
Brazil

LARRY WRIGHT
Detroit News

DARYL
CAGLE
MSNBC.com

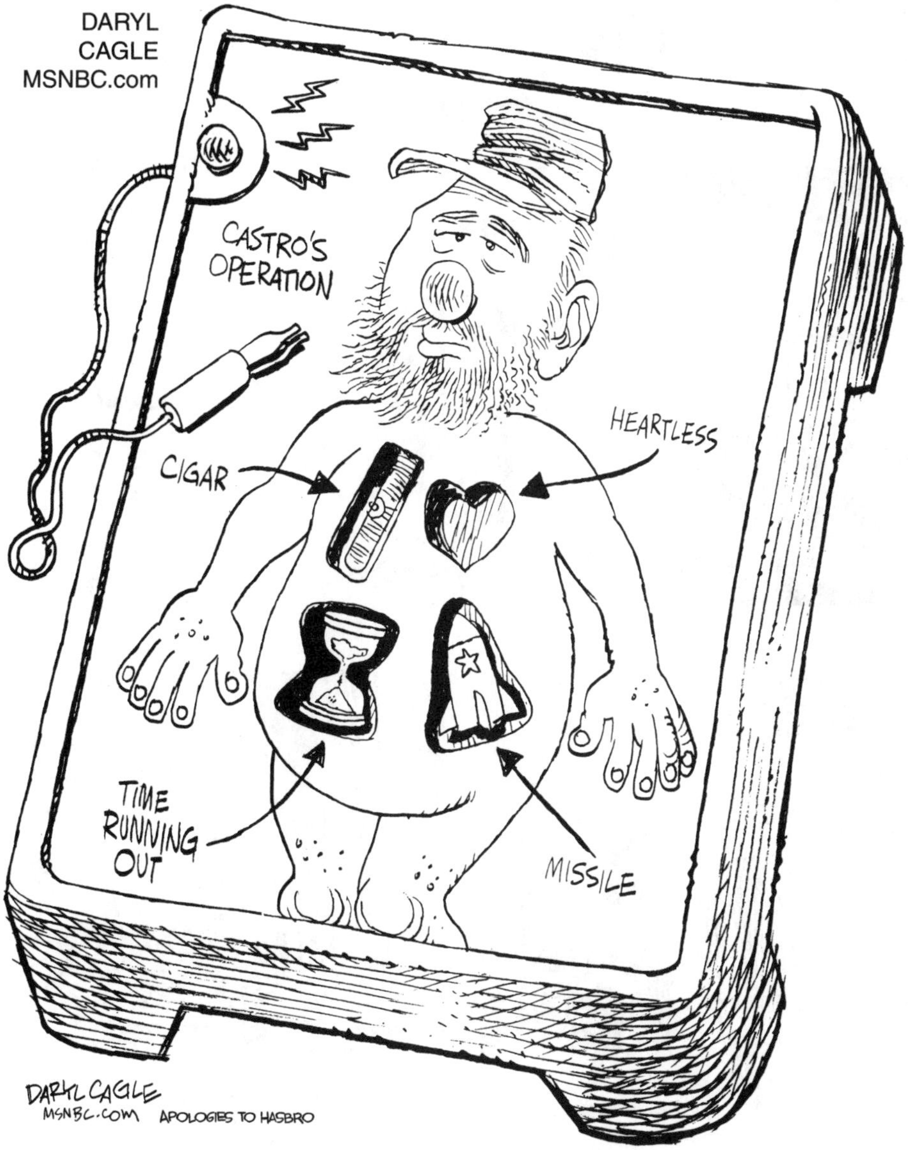

PAT BAGLEY
Salt Lake Tribune

ANTONIO NERIL LICON
Mexico

GARY MARKSTEIN

ED STEIN, Rocky Mountain News

JOHN DARKOW, Columbia Daily Tribune (MO)

MIKE KEEFE, Denver Post

JIMMY MARGULIES, The Record (NJ)

TERRY "AISLIN" MOSHER, Montreal Gazette

GARY VARVEL, Indianapolis Star

JEFF STAHLER
Columbus Disptch

RIBER HANSSON
Sweden

RAINER HACHFELD
Germany

BUT THAT'S ONLY TEMPORARY...

R.CASTRO

CHRISTO KOMARNITSKI, Bulgaria

DARIO CASTILLEJOS, Mexico

STEVE BENSON, Arizona Republic

BILL DAY, Memphis Commercial-Appeal

THOMAS "TAB" BOLDT, Calgary Sun (Canada)

DeLay Steps Down

Despite vehemently proclaiming his innocence, Republican Congressman Tom DeLay was forced to resign from his post as House Majority Leader. The rules of the Republican conference call for members to step down from leadership roles if they are indicted, as DeLay was in 2005. Though the Texan calls the charges against him a "sham" and "political retribution," he's already been found guilty by a jury of editorial cartoonists.

R.J. MATSON
Roll Call

AUCTION ITEMS

SIGNED MUGSHOT AND FINGERPRINT OF INDICTED FORMER* HOUSE MAJORITY LEADER TOM DELAY

UNLIMITED QUANTITIES AVAILABLE!

CURRENT BID: $979,650.00
BUY IT NOW PRICE: $2,000.00

PLACE BID

TIME LEFT: 1 YEAR 14 DAYS
START TIME: OCT. 19, 2005
HISTORY: 3,528,461 Bids
HIGH BIDDER: patriot4DeLay

*AS IF!

SELLER INFORMATION

ARMPAC POSITIVE FEEDBACK: 110%

©MATSON ROLLCALL

NEW STAMP

Tom DeLay

2¢

HIS POLITICAL FUTURE IS WORTH

BOB ENGLEHART
Hartford Courant

FALL DOWN? OH, THAT MUST HURT.

DeLay

DARYL CAGLE
MSNBC.com

DARYL CAGLE MSNBC.com

The self-exterminator

JOHN SHERFFIUS
Boulder Daily Camera

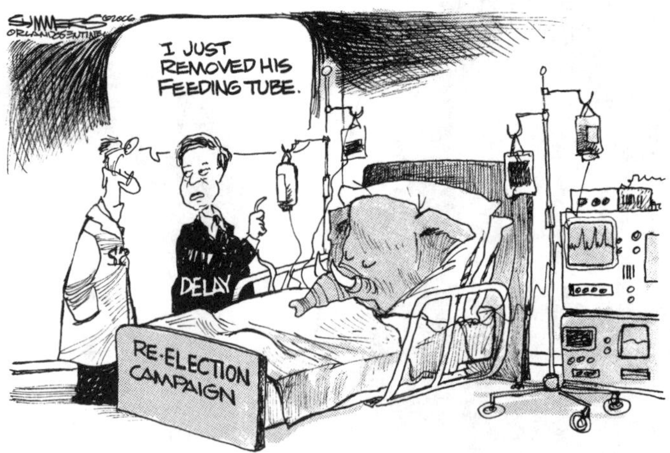

DANA SUMMERS, Orlando Sentinel

"STRANGE THAT A FORMER EXTERMINATOR WOULD INFEST THE WHOLE BUILDING."

JEFF PARKER
Florida Today

PAUL COMBS
Tampa Tribune

ED STEIN, Rocky Mountain News

LARRY WRIGHT, Detroit News

KIRK WALTERS, Toledo Blade

DAN WASSERMAN, Boston Globe

GARY BROOKINS, Richmond Times-Dispatch

White House Press Secretary, Tony Snow

Fox newsman Tony Snow gave up his anchor chair for the White House podium, replacing embattled Scott McClellan as Bush's press secretary. Snow's switch shed even more doubt on *Fox News'* constant claim that they are "fair and balanced"—but most cartoonists weren't terribly surprised.

DARYL CAGLE, MSNBC.com

KIRK WALTER
Toledo Blade

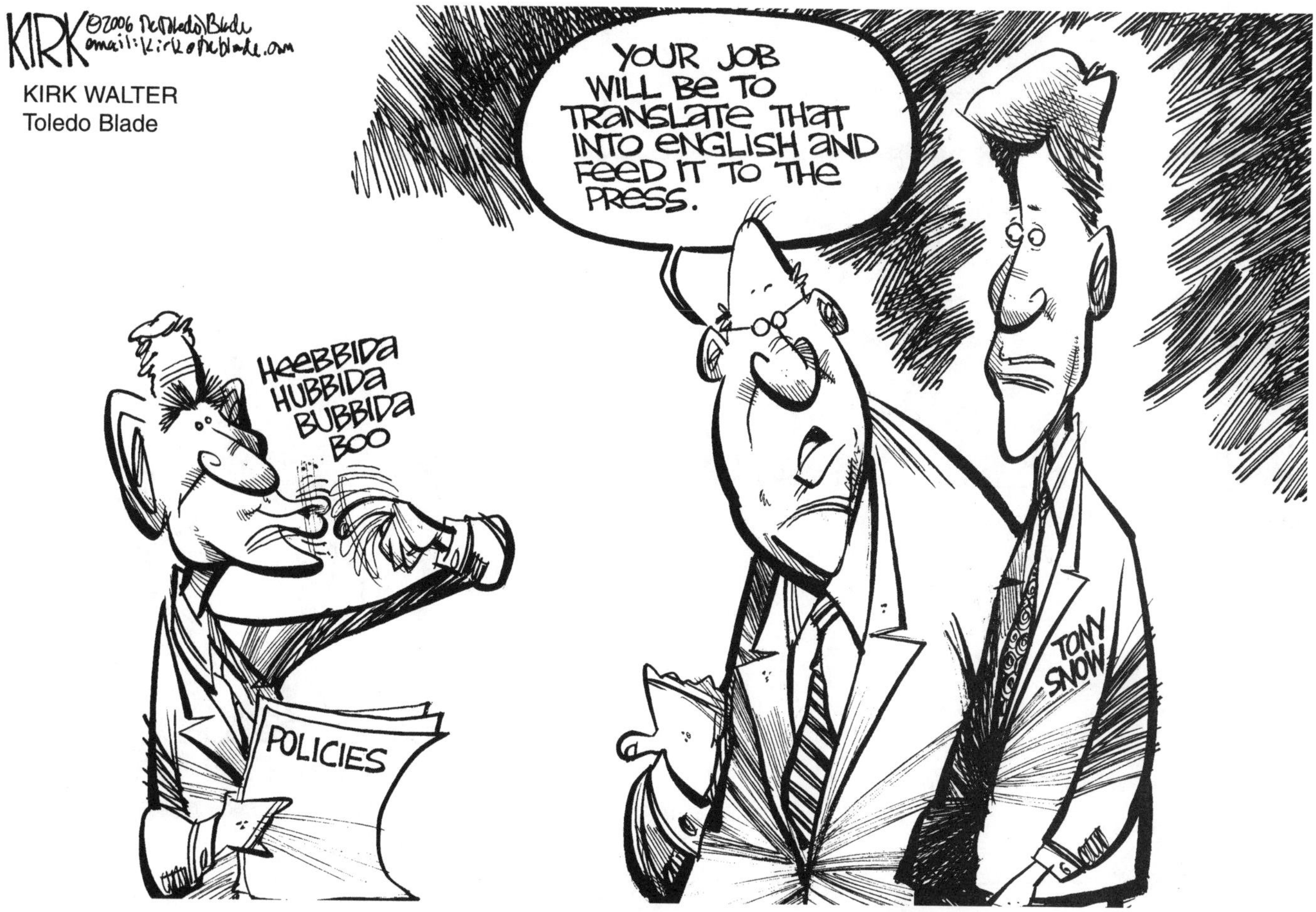
KIRK
YOUR JOB WILL BE TO TRANSLATE THAT INTO ENGLISH AND FEED IT TO THE PRESS.
HEEBBIDA HUBBIDA BUBBIDA BOO
POLICIES
TONY SNOW

JOHN BRANCH
San Antonio
Express-News

SECOND TERM SPIN CYCLE
TONY SNOW
New Improved PR!!!
RUMSFELD
the WAR
GAS PRICES
DOMESTIC SPYING
CHENEY
IRAN
BRANCH
SAN ANTONIO EXPRESS-NEWS

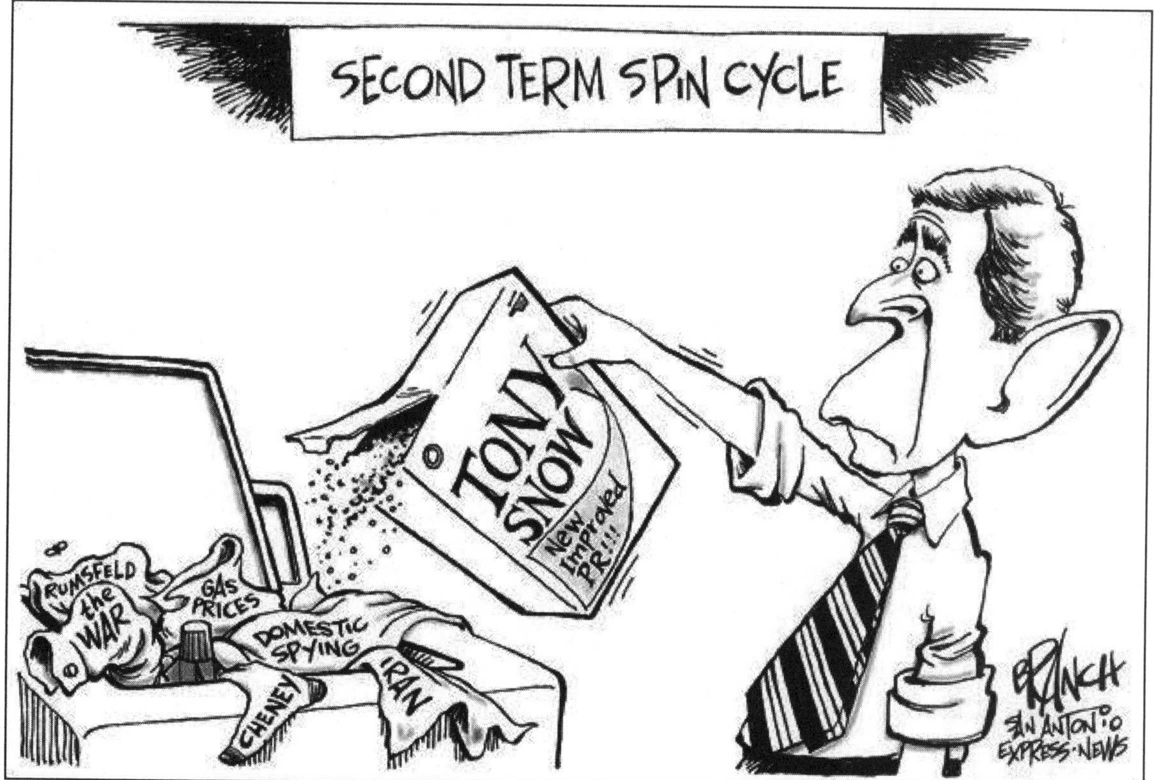

I'M NOT A CALLER! I'M SITTING RIGHT HERE!
caglecartoons.com
TONY SNOW

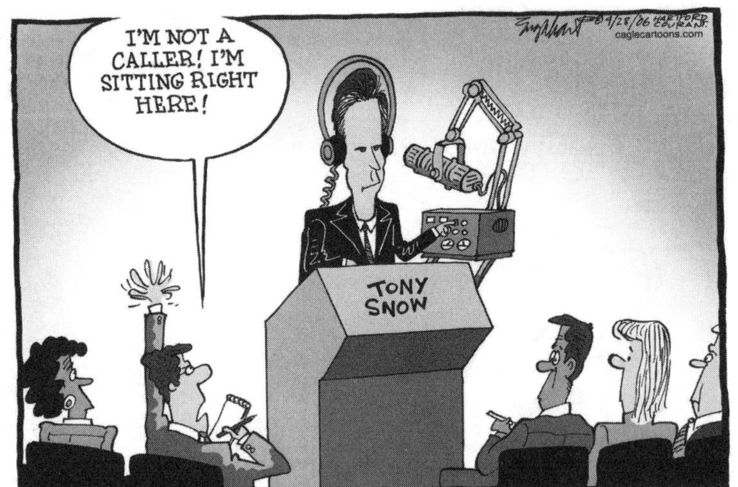

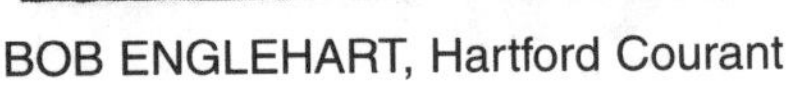

BOB ENGLEHART, Hartford Courant

BILL DAY
Memphis Commercial Appeal

The Snow Job
HERO
Tony

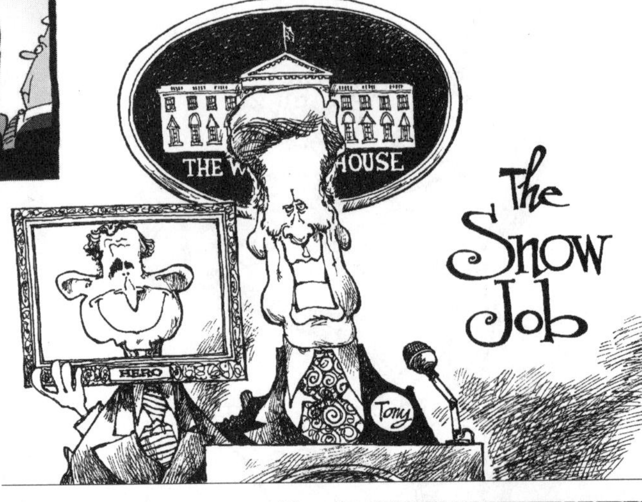

NATE BEELER, Washington Examiner

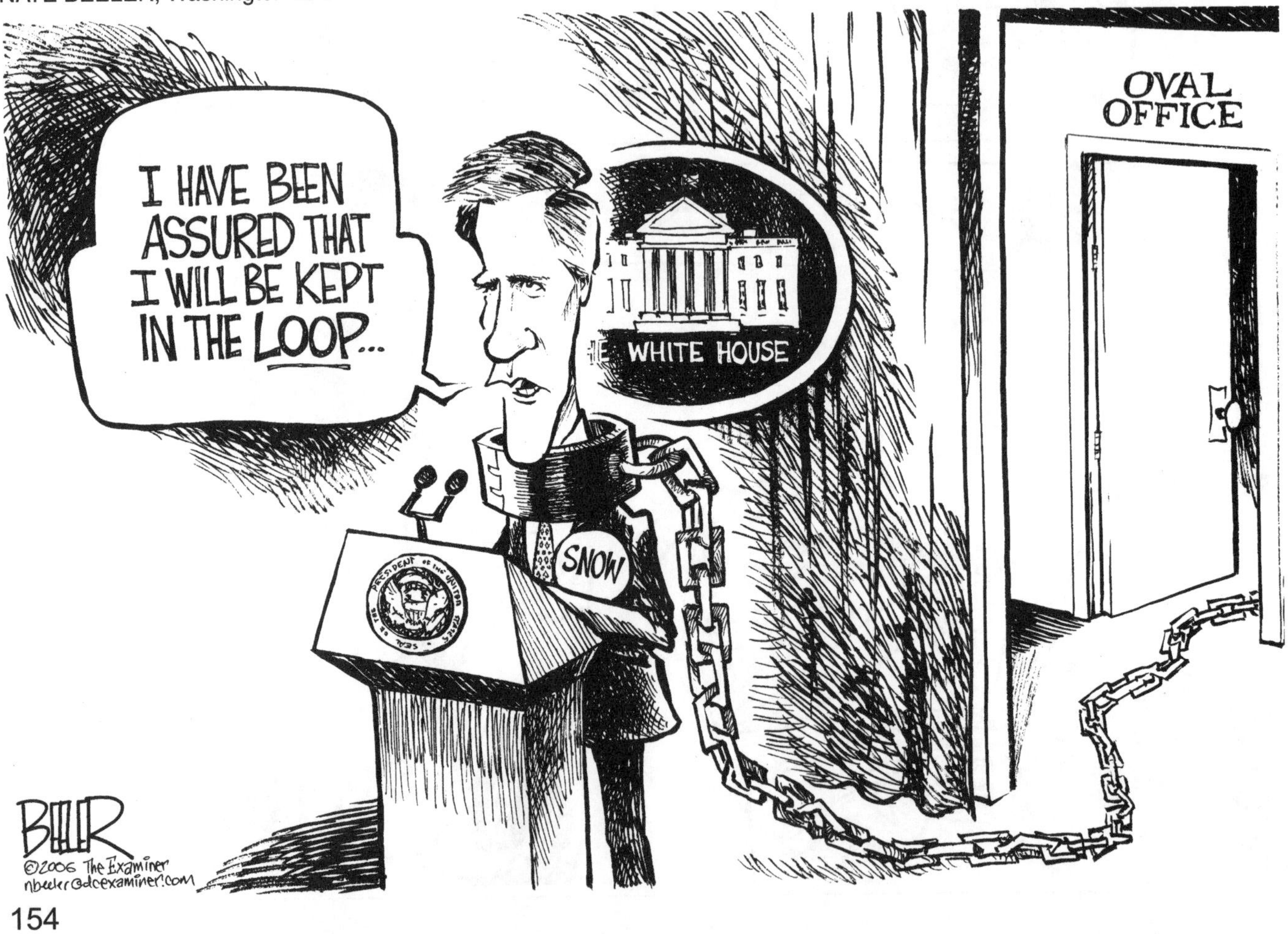

I HAVE BEEN ASSURED THAT I WILL BE KEPT IN THE LOOP...
WHITE HOUSE
OVAL OFFICE
SNOW
BEELER
©2006 The Examiner
nbeeler@dcexaminer.com

SANDY HUFFAKER
Cagle Cartoons

JOE HELLER
Green Bay Press-Gazette

FOX NEWS

TONY SNOW GOES TO THE WHITE HOUSE

RECEPTIONIST

"I'M SORRY BUT MR. SNOW NO LONGER WORKS HERE... HE WAS PROMOTED TO CORPORATE HEADQUARTERS LAST WEEK!"

MIKE THOMPSON
Detroit Free-Press

SCOTT STANTIS
Birmingham News

WHITE HOUSE PRESS ROOM
SNOW
©2006 TREVER ALBUQUERQUE JOURNAL

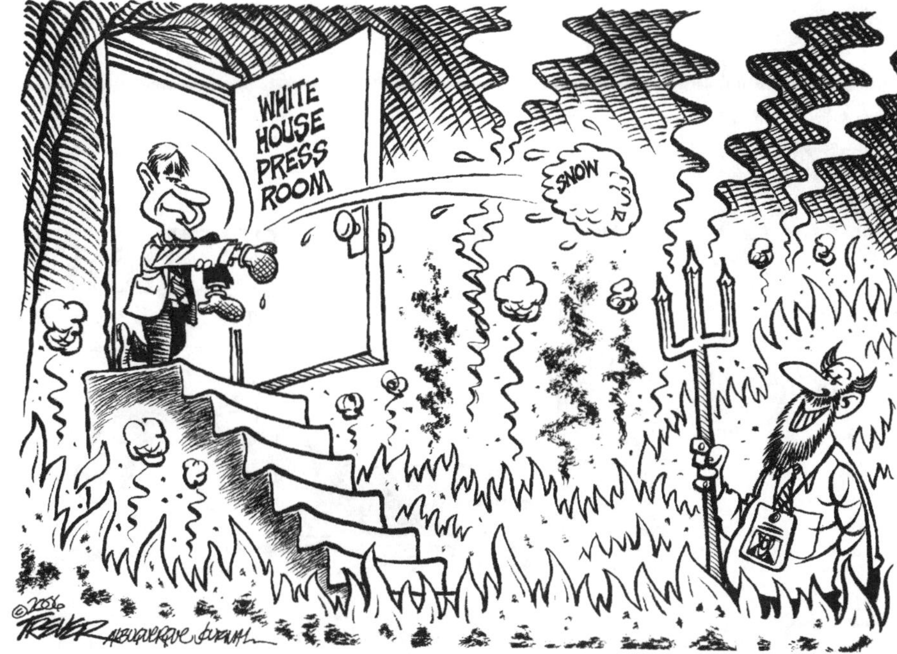

JOHN TREVER
Albuquerque Journal

JOHN DARKOW
Columbia Daily Tribune (MO)

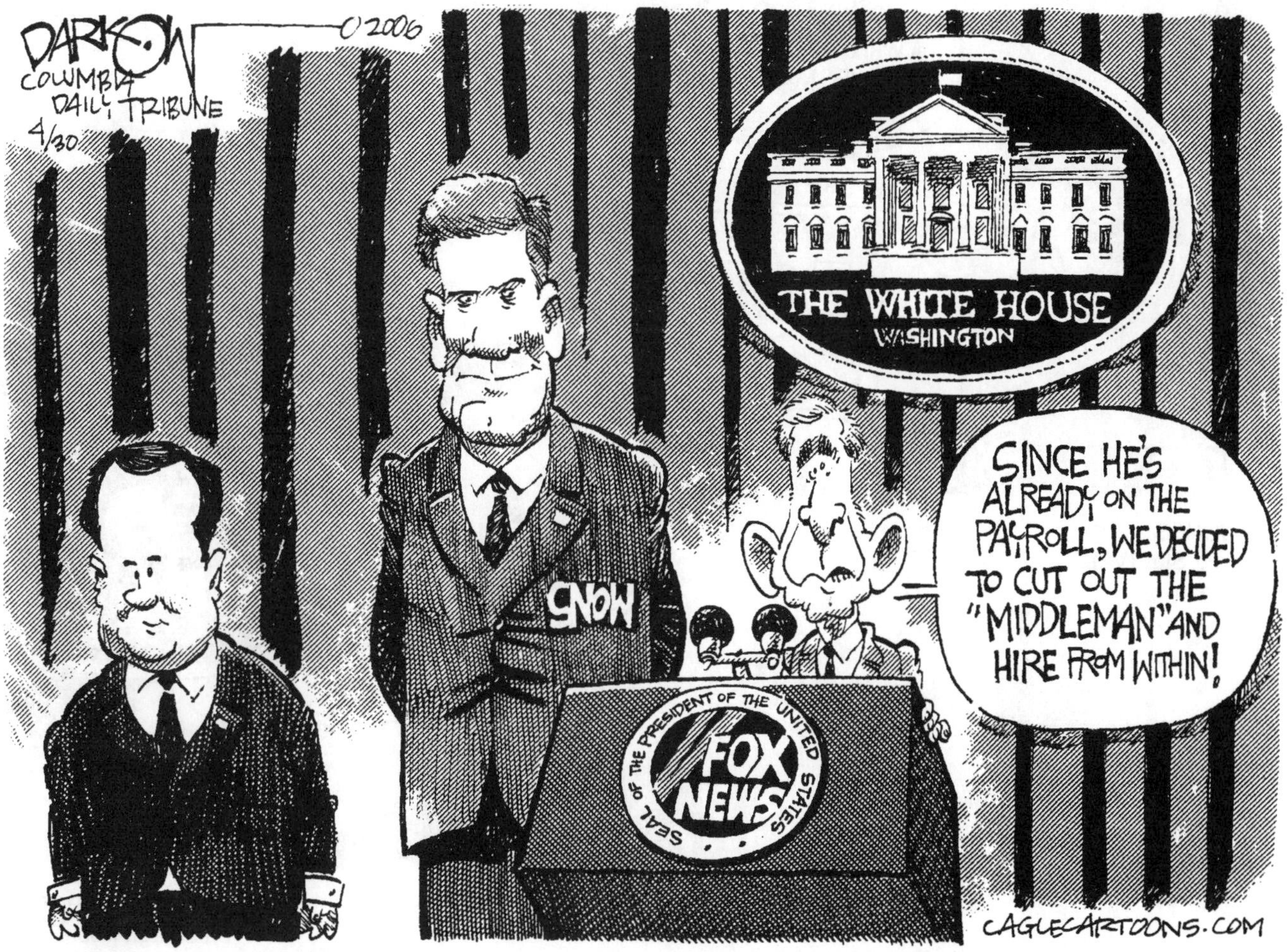
DARKOW ©2006
COLUMBIA DAILY TRIBUNE 4/30
THE WHITE HOUSE
WASHINGTON
SINCE HE'S ALREADY ON THE PAYROLL, WE DECIDED TO CUT OUT THE "MIDDLEMAN" AND HIRE FROM WITHIN!
SNOW
SEAL OF THE PRESIDENT OF THE UNITED STATES
FOX NEWS
CAGLECARTOONS.COM

CHIP BOK
Akron Beacon-Journal

"Well, he got a new microphone. That's a start."

HENRY PAYNE
Detroit News

CLAY JONES
Freelance-Star (VA)

ROB ROGERS
Pittsburgh Post-Gazette

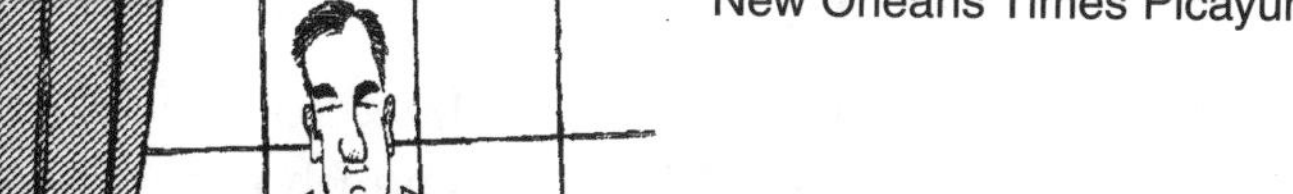

STEVE KELLEY
New Orleans Times Picayune

STEVE BENSON
Arizona Republic

Foley's Foibles

Florida Republican Congressman Mark Foley found himself at the center of the biggest political sex scandal since Bill and Monica, when he was discovered to have sent sexually explicit e-mails to underage congressional pages. Foley resigned from Congress and claimed he is gay, was molested by a Catholic priest as a boy, and was checking into a rehabilitation clinic for alcoholism. It's a well-known equation:
politician + sex scandal + resulting emotional breakdown = an editorial cartoonist's dream come true.

MIKE LESTER, Rome News-Tribune (GA)

DARYL CAGLE
MSNBC.com

CHAN LOWE, South Florida Sun-Sentinel

DANA SUMMERS, Orlando Sentinel

AARON TAYLOR, Provo (UT) Daily Herald

ADAM ZYGLIS, Buffalo News

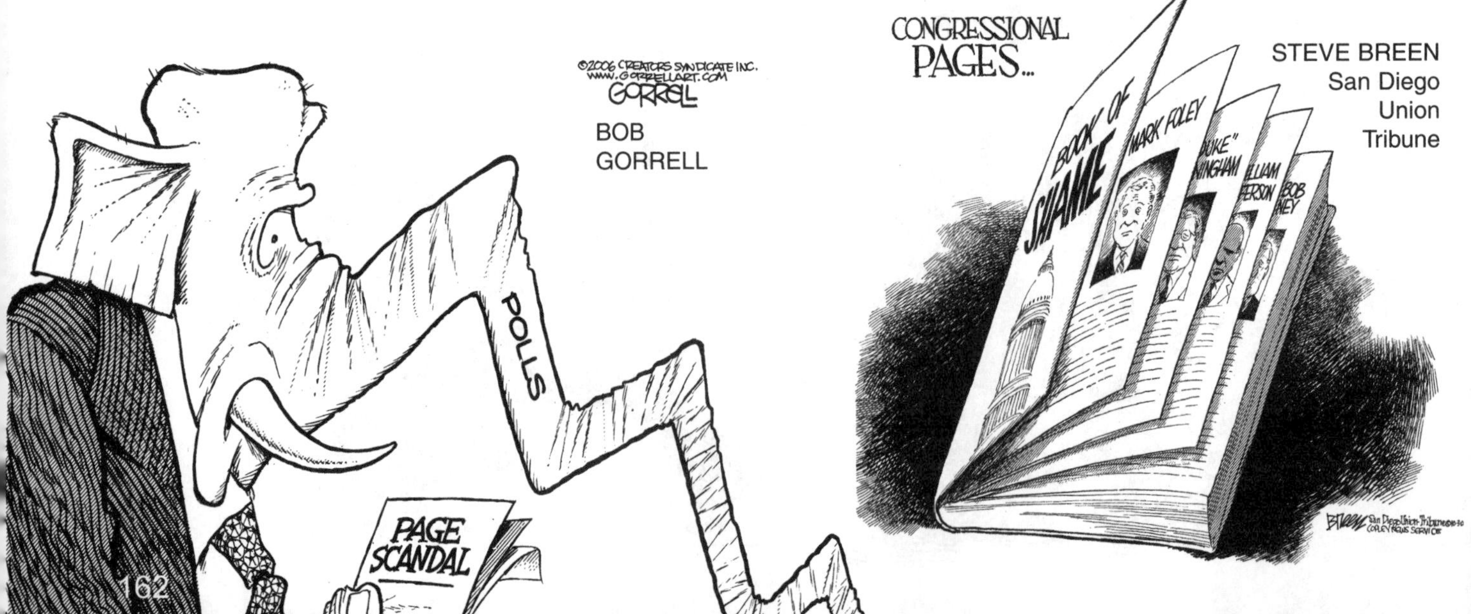

BOB GORRELL

STEVE BREEN San Diego Union Tribune

WALT HANDELSMAN
Newsday

R.J. MATSON
St. Louis Post Dispatch

"SOME CONGRESSMAN FROM FLORIDA WANTS TO KNOW IF HE'S MAKING ME HORNY!"

GARY MARKSTEIN

JOHN COLE, Scranton Times-Tribune

MIKE KEEFE, Denver Post

CHRIS BRITT, State Journal-Register

CHIP BOK, Akron Beacon-Journal

CHRIS BRITT, State Journal-Register (IL)

caglecartoons.com
LARRY WRIGHT
Detroit News

ROBERT ARIAIL
The State (SC)

GARY BROOKINS, Richmond Times-Dispatch

JOHN BRANCH, San Antonio Express News

HENRY PAYNE, Detroit News

STEVE SACK, Minneapolis Star Tribune

SCOTT STANTIS, Birmingham News

MILT PRIGGEE, Politicalcartoons.com

STEVE BREEN
San Diego Union Tribune

MIKE LESTER, Rome News Tribune (GA)

JIMMY MARGULIES
The Record (NJ)

KEVIN SIERS, Charlotte Observer

Domestic Spying

This year *The New York Times* broke the story that the executive branch's National Security Agency had been performing secret warrantless electronic surveillance since shortly after September 11, 2001. A few months later, a U.S. District judge ruled the program unconstitutional. Cartoonists were as shocked and awed as the rest of the country—which is to say, they've come to expect this from the Bush administration.

BRIAN FAIRRINGTON, Cagle Cartoons

ELECTRONIC EAVESDROPPING IN A NORMAN ROCKWELLIAN, ORWELLIAN AMERICA

R.J. MATSON
St. Louis
Post-Dispatch

ROBERT ARIAIL
The State (SC)

M.e. Cohen/HumorInk.com 01.25

The Democrats don't care about your safety. They don't want me to eavesdrop on terrorists living in America!

No. That's not true. We want you to eavesdrop on terrorists wherever they are. Just get a court order first.

In fact, the way the FISA court is set up you don't even have to get a court order first. Just within 72 hours after you've begun to wiretap.

The Democrats are soft on terrorism.

No. That's not the truth. Please, please eavesdrop on terrorists now. Just follow the law.

The Democrats would rather see us all killed by terrorists than eavesdrop.

No. Tell the truth. The Constitution outlines checks and balances to insure our freedoms. But please eavesdrop on terrorists now. Just follow the law.

The Democrats are pussies!

Stop. Have you heard anything that I've said?

I only hear what I can eavesdrop.

M.e. COHEN, Politicalcartoons.com

JACK OHMAN, Portland Oregonian

PAT BAGLEY, Salt Lake Tribune (UT)

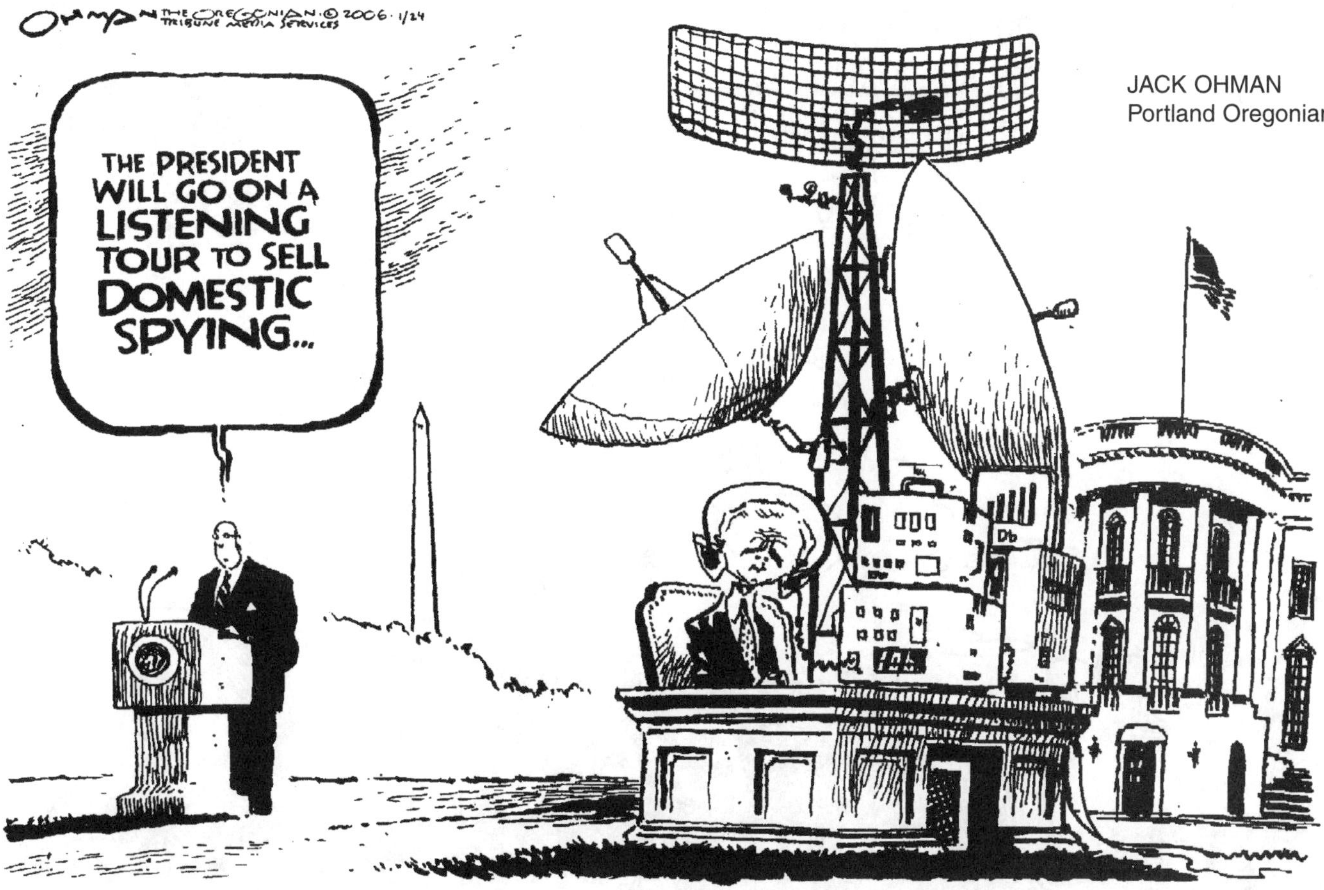

OHMAN THE OREGONIAN ©2006 1/24 TRIBUNE MEDIA SERVICES

THE PRESIDENT WILL GO ON A LISTENING TOUR TO SELL DOMESTIC SPYING...

JACK OHMAN
Portland Oregonian

CHAN LOWE, South Florida Sun-Sentinel

ROB ROGERS, Pittsburgh Post-Gazette

JEFF PARKER, Florida Today

WAYNE STAYSKAL

JEFF PARKER, Florida Today

CHRISTO KOMARNITSKI, Bulgaria

DOUG MARLETTE, Tulsa World

MATT DAVIES, Journal News (NY)

"He's a government surveillance expert here to keep us safe!"

DANA SUMMERS
Orlando Sentinel

PAT BAGLEY, Salt Lake Tribune (UT)

MATT DAVIES
Journal News (NY)

"YOU REALLY SHOULDN'T VISIT THAT ADULT WEBSITE, AND LET'S CUT BACK ON PHONE CALLS TO PEOPLE WITH HYPHENATED LAST NAMES."

BOB GORRELL

MIKE LANE, Cagle Cartoons

STEVE SACK, Minneapolis Star-Tribune

STAR TRIBUNE
SACK

spyPod

ILLEGAL DOMESTIC WIRETAPS

DWANE POWELL, Raliegh News & Observer

MATT DAVIES, Journal News (NY)

MIKE LANE, Cagle Cartoons

ROB ROGERS
Pittsburgh Post-Gazette

CORKY TRINIDAD
Honolulu Star Bulletin

NSA

CORKY '06
STAR-BULLETIN

"JUST CAME TO THANK YOU GUYS FOR A FINE JOB YOU'RE DOING... HEY!...IS...THAT...JENNA?!?..."

OLLE JOHANSSON, Sweden

AS A RIGHT-THINKING AMERICAN I RESENT THE COMMIE LEFT REVEALING BUSH'S DOMESTIC SPYING PROGRAM!!

...DID YOU GET THAT, MR. PRESIDENT?

MIKE LANE, Cagle Cartoons

THE ILLEGAL N.S.A. SECRET WIRETAPS AUTHORIZED BY THE BUSH ADMINISTRATION DESTROY OUR AMERICAN FREEDOMS AND INVADE OUR PRIVACY!

YO, DUDE- I'M ON THE PHONE!

THAT'S LIKE TOTALLY WHACK, MAN.

MIKE LESTER, Rome News-Tribune (GA)

LARRY WRIGHT
Detroit News

Bush Leaks

Bush's press secretary, Scott McClellan, claimed no one in the Bush administration had leaked the identity of CIA agent Valerie Plame, and Bush himself made strong remarks on the Plame leak: Anyone in his administration who was outed as a leaker, he claimed, would be fired. But when Vice President Cheney's aide "Scooter" Libby was outed as the leaker, Bush backpedaled. Cartoonists were split into two cynical camps: "big surprise" and "big deal."

JOHN SHERFFIUS
Boulder Daily Camera

"If there's a leak out of my administration, I want to know who it is."
– President Bush

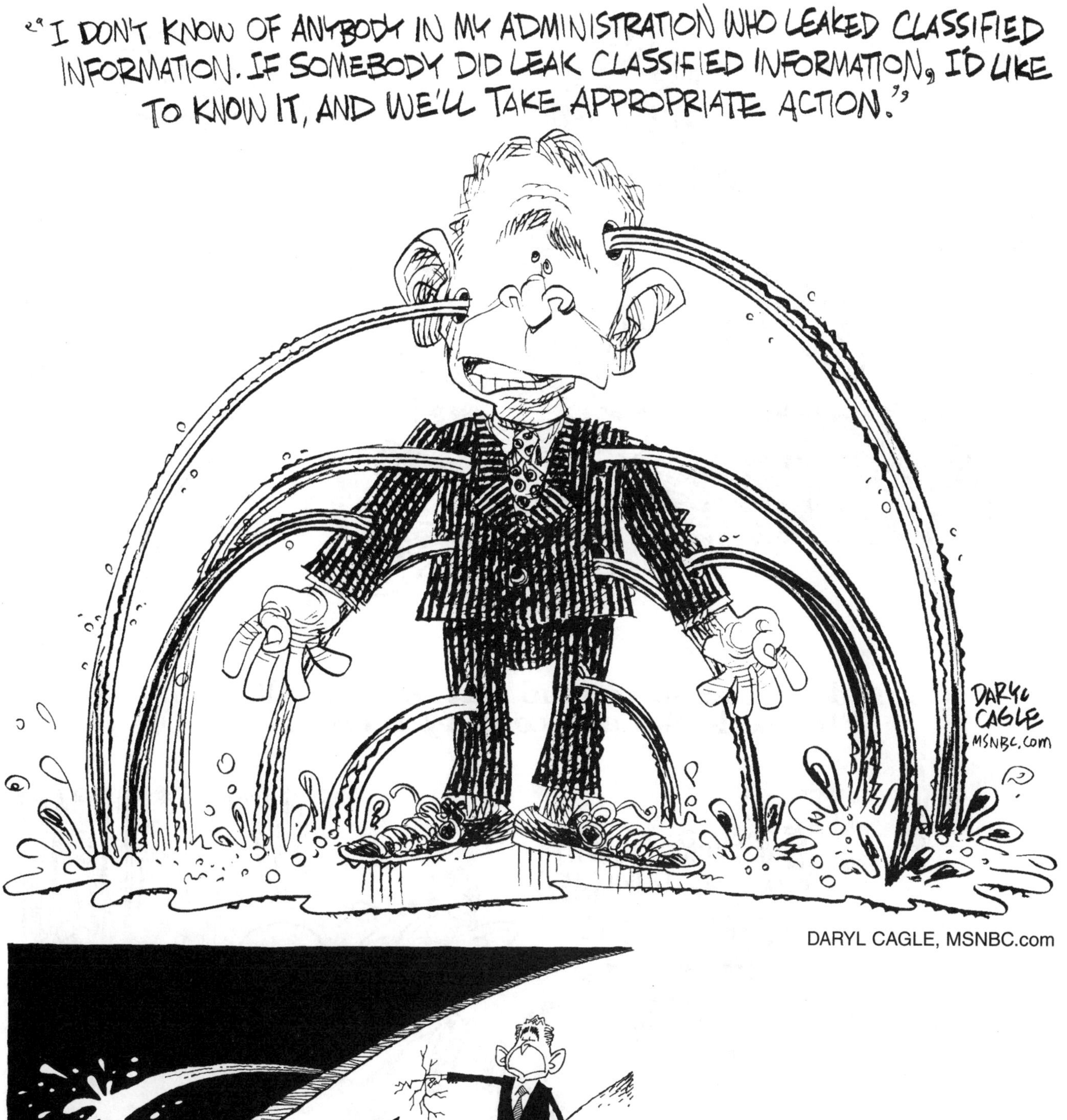
"I DON'T KNOW OF ANYBODY IN MY ADMINISTRATION WHO LEAKED CLASSIFIED INFORMATION. IF SOMEBODY DID LEAK CLASSIFIED INFORMATION, I'D LIKE TO KNOW IT, AND WE'LL TAKE APPROPRIATE ACTION."
DARYL CAGLE MSNBC.com

DARYL CAGLE, MSNBC.com

CREDIBILITY
edStein '06 Rocky Mtn. News·Nea

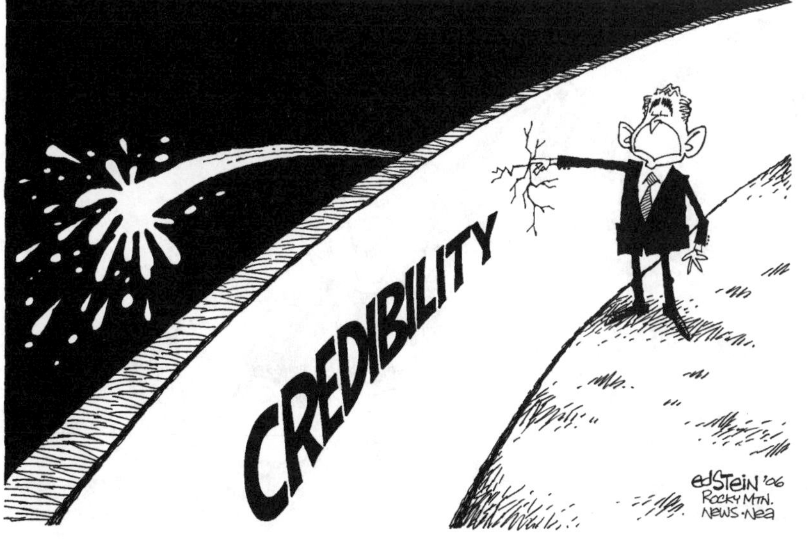

ED STEIN
Rocky Mountain News

JIMMY MARGULIES
The Record (NJ)

hypocrisy

"I'm determined to find out where all these leaks are coming from..."

MIKE LANE
Cagle Cartoons

BOB ENGLEHART, Hartford Courant

ANY LUCK IDENTIFYING THE SOURCE OF THOSE LEAKS?...

STEVE SACK
Minneapolis Star-Tribune

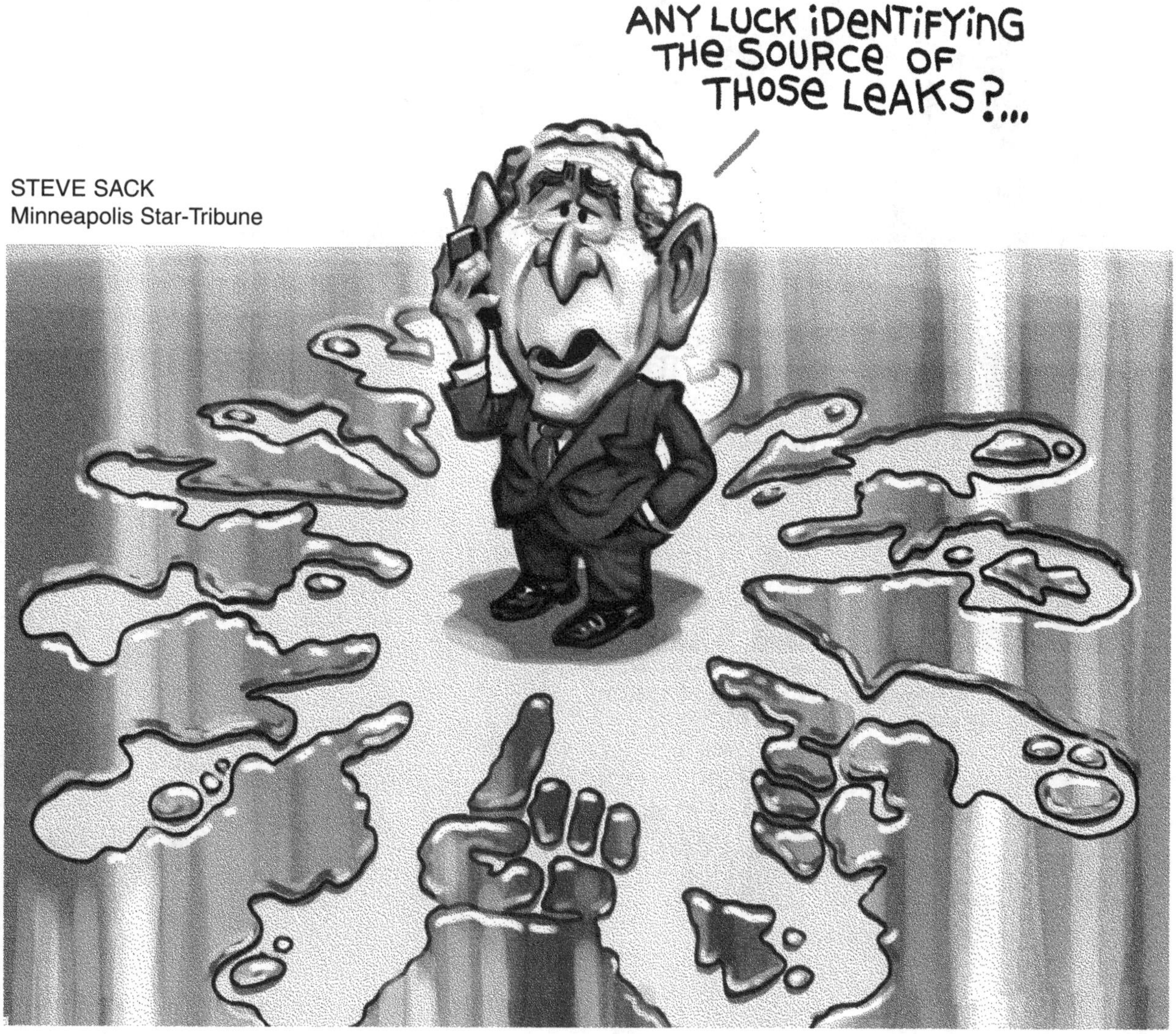

JEFF PARKER
Florida Today

caglecartoons.com

DAN WASSERMAN, Boston Globe

JOHN COLE, Scranton Times-Tribune

BUSH LEAKS

JOE HELLER
Green Bay Press-Gazette

GOSPEL OF
Judas
ANCIENT
MANUSC

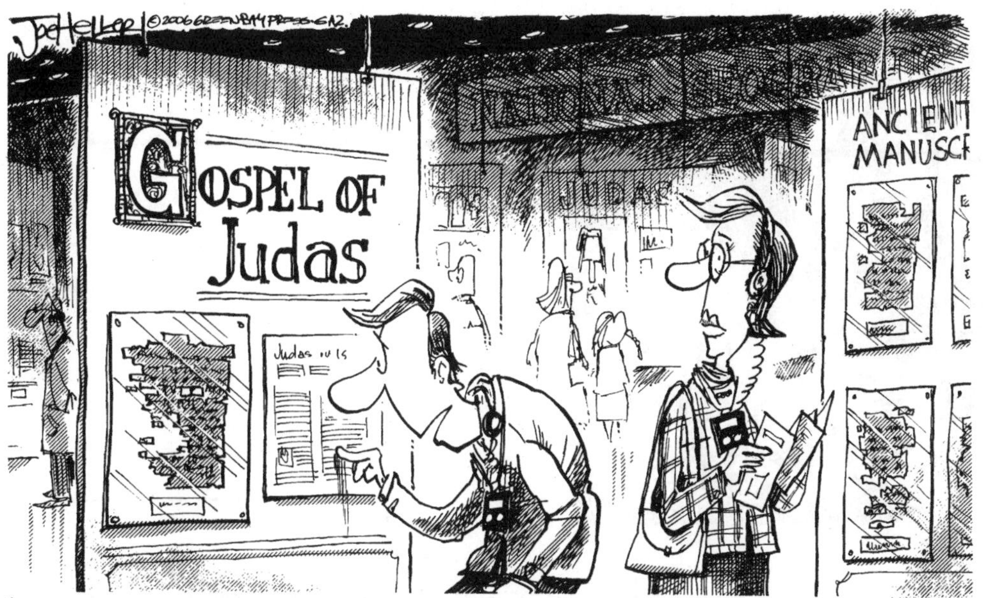

"ROUGHLY TRANSLATED, IT SAYS, NO ONE WAS BETRAYED BECAUSE 'SCOOTER' LIBBY ONLY LEAKED THE INFORMATION THE PRESIDENT WANTED HIM TO!"

GARY MARKSTEIN

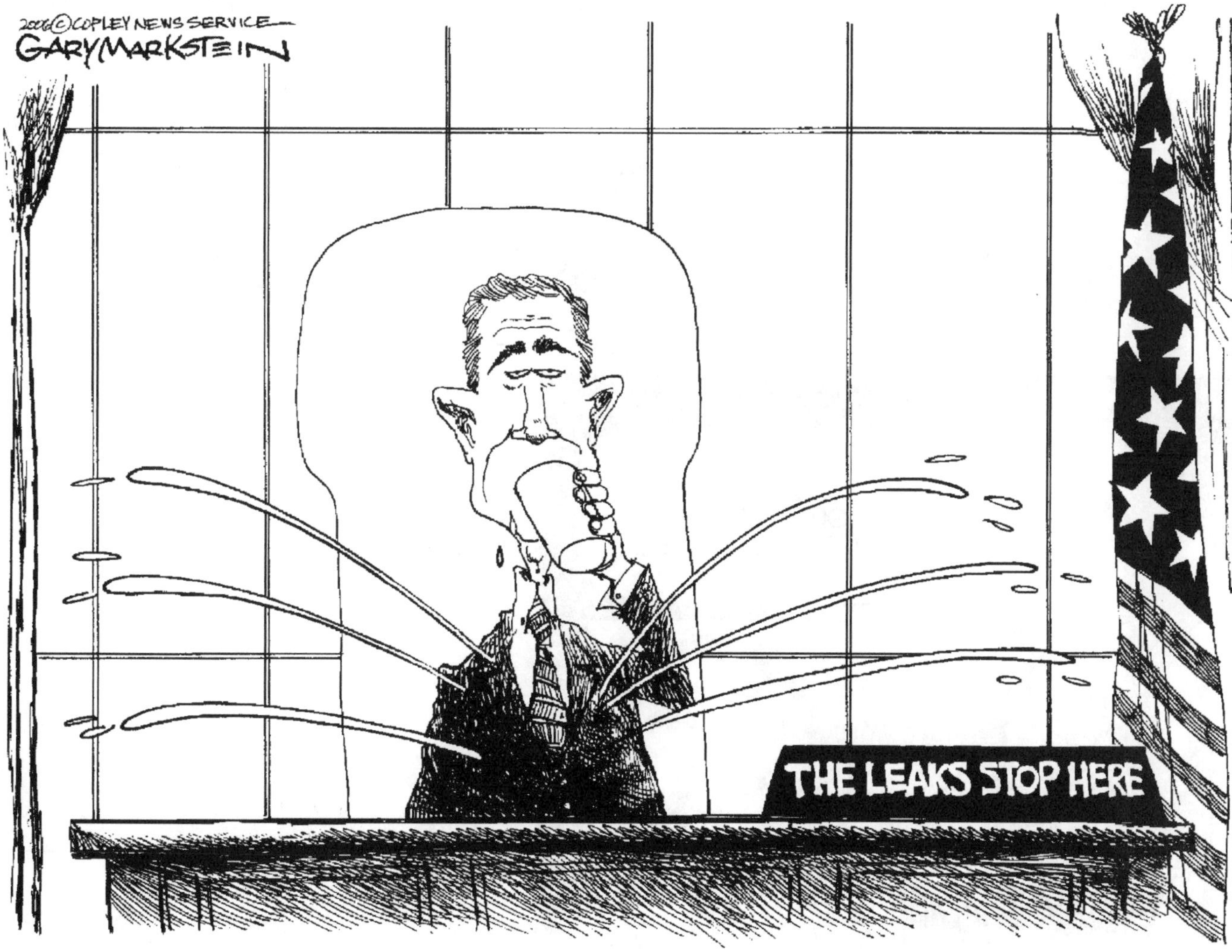
2006 © COPLEY NEWS SERVICE
GARY MARKSTEIN
THE LEAKS STOP HERE

JACK OHMAN
Portland Oregonian

CHRIS BRITT
State Journal-Register (IL)

STEVE BREEN
San Diego Union-Tribune

GARY MARKSTEIN

ROBERT ARIAIL
The State (SC)

KEVIN SIERS
Charlotte Observer

MATT DAVIES
Journal News, NY

VIC HARVILLE
Stephens Media Group

GUY BADEAUX
Journal Le Droit, Canada

NICK ANDERSON
Houston Chronicle

CLAY JONES, Freelance-Star, VA

STEVE KELLEY
New Orleans
Times-Picayune

KEN CATALINO

MONTE WOLVERTON, Cagle Cartoons

LARRY WRIGHT, Detroit News

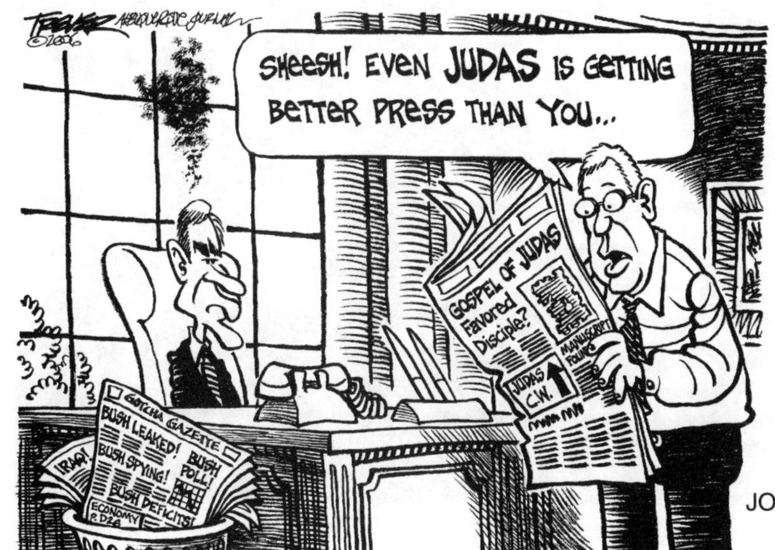

JOHN TREVER, Albuquerque Journal

Lebanon

The crisis in the Middle East took a turn for the worse this year when Lebanon's Iran-backed terrorist group, Hezbollah, kidnapped two Israeli soldiers. As Israel bombed Lebanon to shreds, Hezbollah fought back with guerilla tactics and hundreds of Iranian missiles rained on northern Israel. Cartoonists wondered if there would ever be an end to the conflict.

DWAYNE BOOTH, Mr. Fish

DARYL CAGLE
MSNBC.com

...THE MISSILE DEFENSE SYSTEM HAS BEEN ROLLED INTO POSITION.

DARYL CAGLE
MSNBC.COM

R.J. MATSON
St. Louis Post Dispatch

MICHAEL GRASTON
Windsor Star
Canada

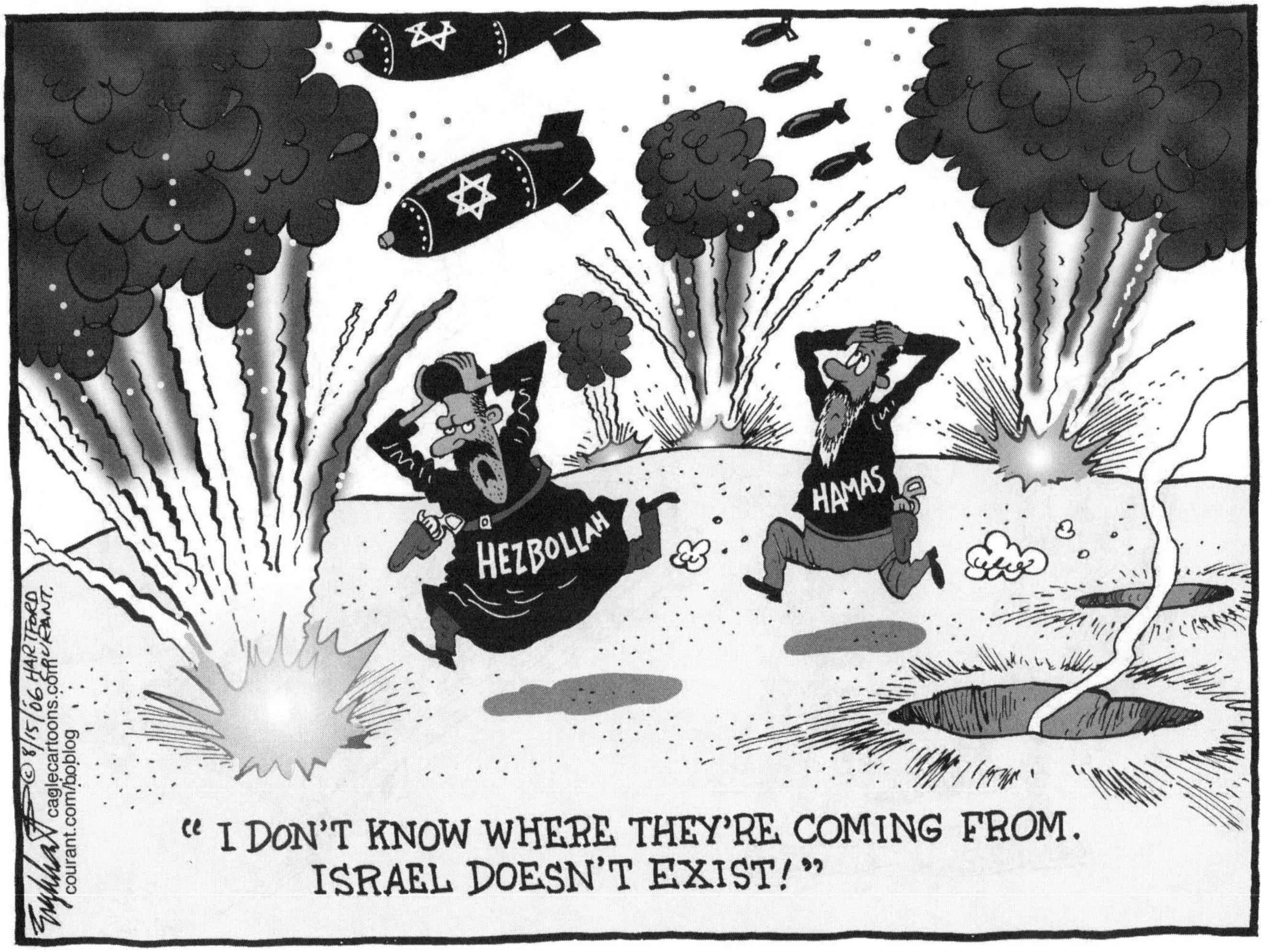
HEZBOLLAH
HAMAS
" I DON'T KNOW WHERE THEY'RE COMING FROM. ISRAEL DOESN'T EXIST! "
© 8/15/06 HARTFORD COURANT.
caglecartoons.com
courant.com/boblog

BOB ENGLEHART, Hartford Courant

HEZBOLLAH...
THE PARTY OF GOD?
©2006 CREATORS SYNDICATE, INC.

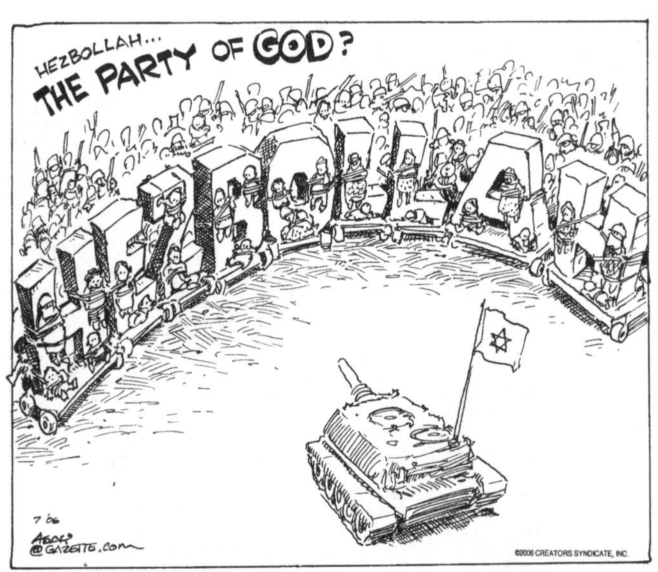

CHUCK ASAY, Colorado Springs Gazette

PEACE
SYRIA
HEZBOLLAH
GAZA
SAUDIS
IRAQ
ISRAEL
IRAN
PEACE
SUNNIS
PEACE
HAMAS
SYRIA
LEBANON
SHIITES
PEACE
US
©2006 CHICAGO TRIBUNE

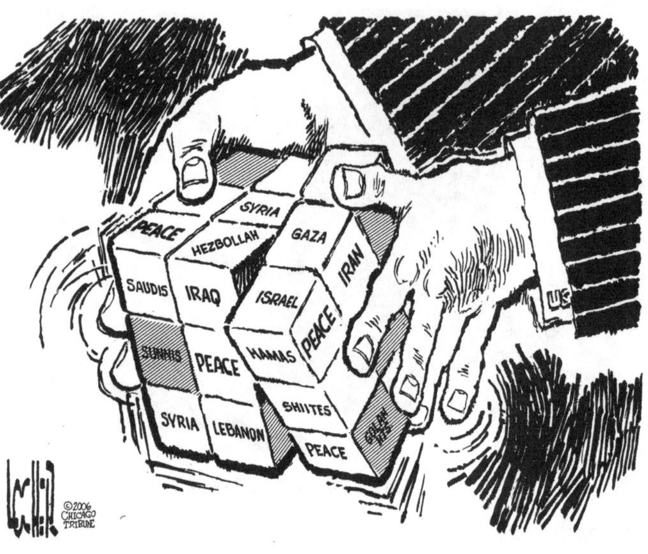

DICK LOCHER, Chicago Tribune

PETAR PISMETROVIC, Austria
UN
HESBOLLAH
OIL
HENRY PAYNE, Detroit News
DICTIONARY OF THE MIDDLE EAST
ISRAEL
"WHAT'S THE HEZBOLLAH WORD FOR 'CEASEFIRE?'.... 'RELOAD.'"

JOE HELLER
Green Bay
Press-Gazette

PAT BAGLEY
Salt Lake Tribune (UT)

JOHN DEERING, Arkansas Democrat Gazette

MARTYN TURNER
Irish Times

DARYL CAGLE
MSNBC.com

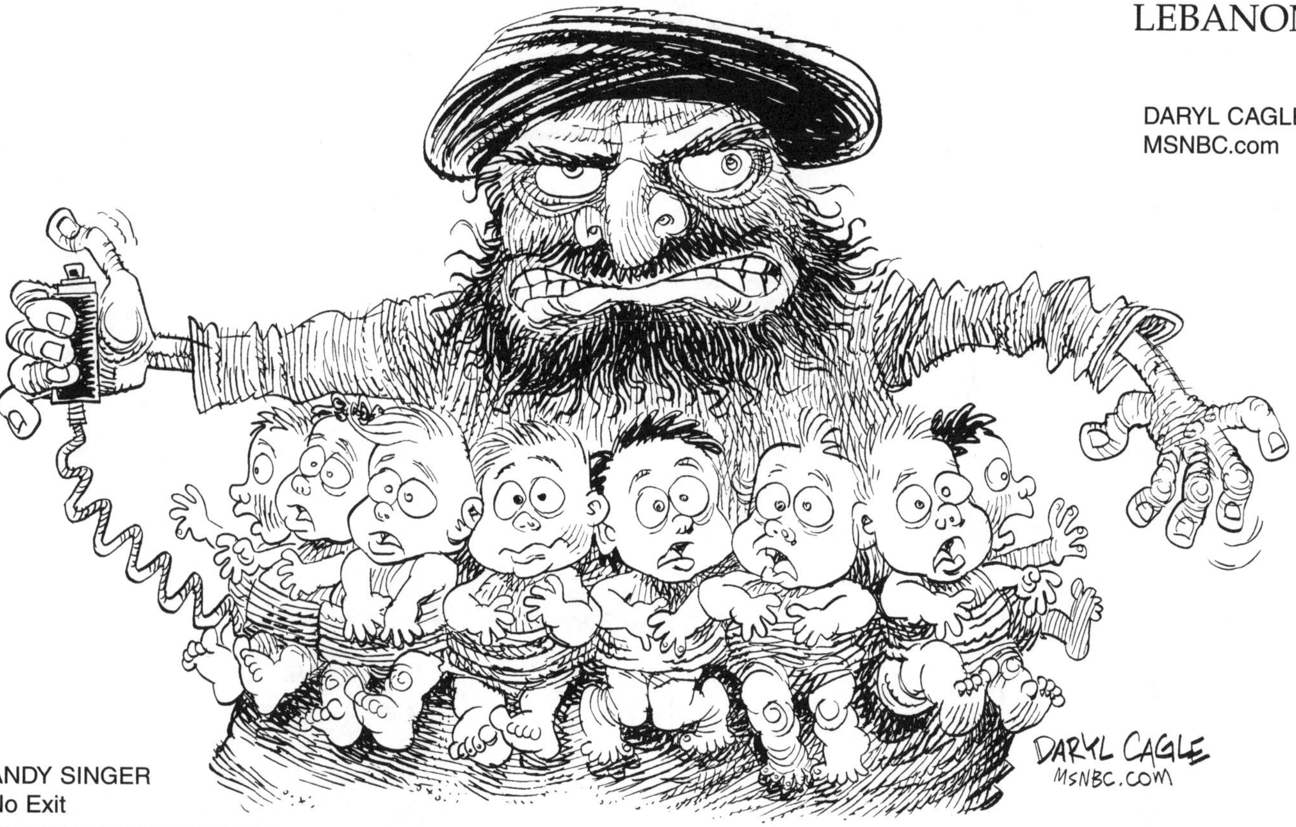
DARYL CAGLE
MSNBC.COM

ANDY SINGER
No Exit

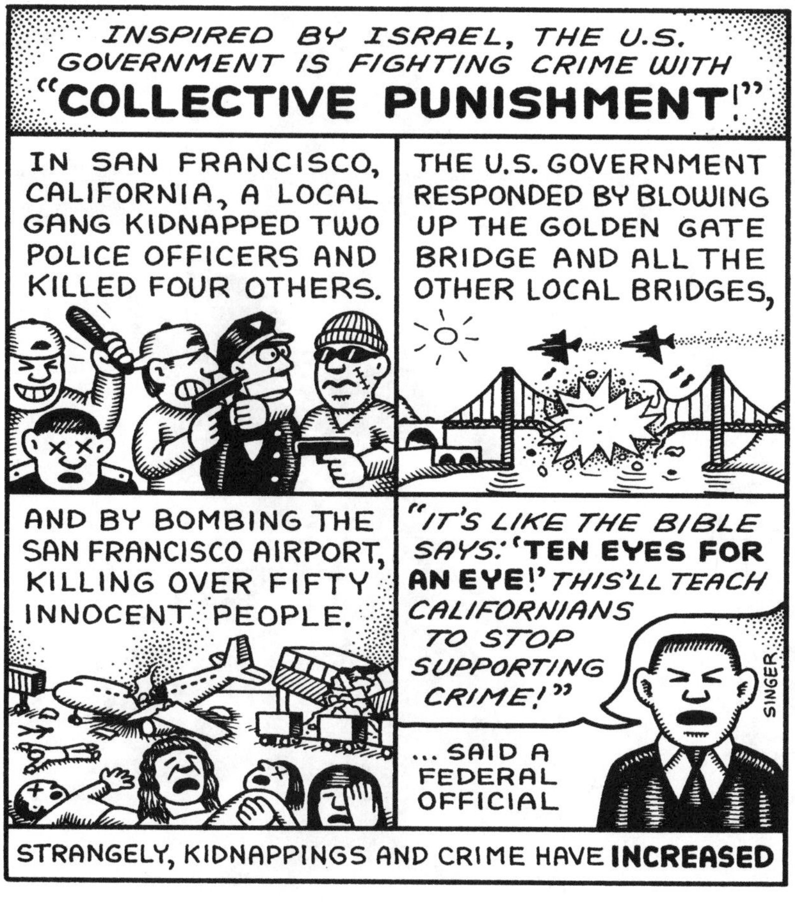
INSPIRED BY ISRAEL, THE U.S. GOVERNMENT IS FIGHTING CRIME WITH "COLLECTIVE PUNISHMENT!"
IN SAN FRANCISCO, CALIFORNIA, A LOCAL GANG KIDNAPPED TWO POLICE OFFICERS AND KILLED FOUR OTHERS.
THE U.S. GOVERNMENT RESPONDED BY BLOWING UP THE GOLDEN GATE BRIDGE AND ALL THE OTHER LOCAL BRIDGES,
AND BY BOMBING THE SAN FRANCISCO AIRPORT, KILLING OVER FIFTY INNOCENT PEOPLE.
"IT'S LIKE THE BIBLE SAYS: 'TEN EYES FOR AN EYE!' THIS'LL TEACH CALIFORNIANS TO STOP SUPPORTING CRIME!"
...SAID A FEDERAL OFFICIAL
SINGER
STRANGELY, KIDNAPPINGS AND CRIME HAVE INCREASED

YAAKOV KIRSCHEN
Jerusalem Post, Israel

Dry Bones NEXT STEPS
THE LEBANESE GOV'T SAYS THAT 15,000 LEBANESE SOLDIERS
WILL BE SENT TO PATROL SOUTH LEBANON.
EITHER THAT OR THEY'LL JUST SEND 15,000 UNIFORMS
AND LET THE HEZBOLLAH TERRORISTS WEAR THEM.
NEWS
NEWS
NEWS
NEWS
©06 Kirschen

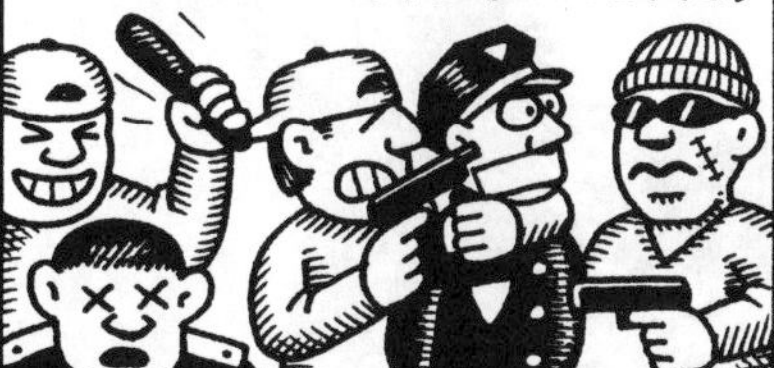

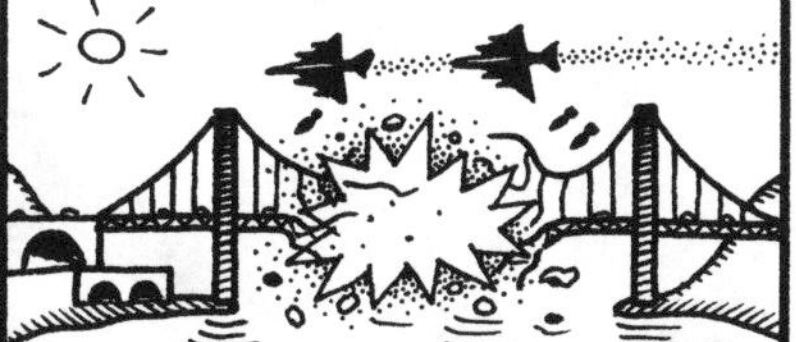

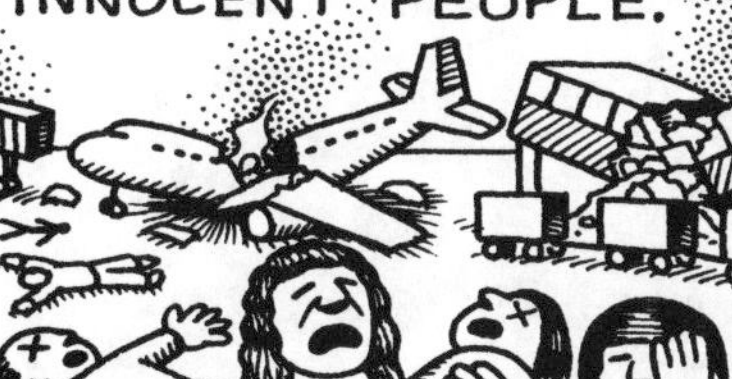

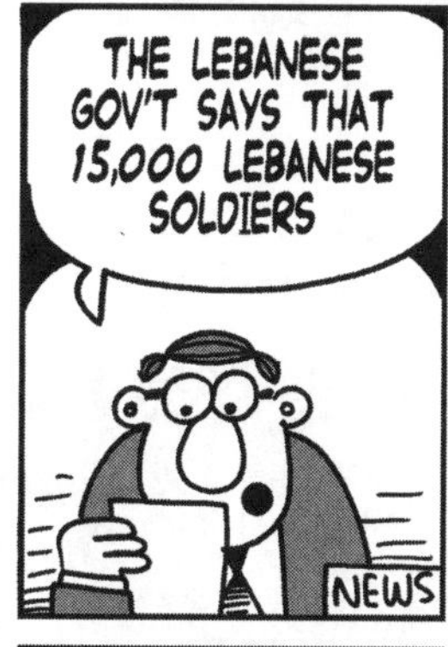

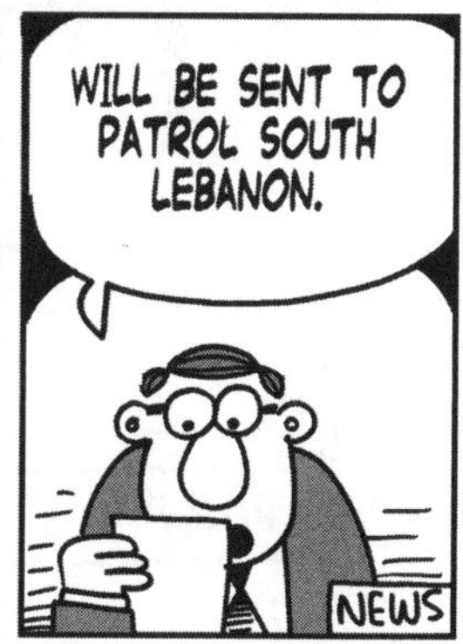

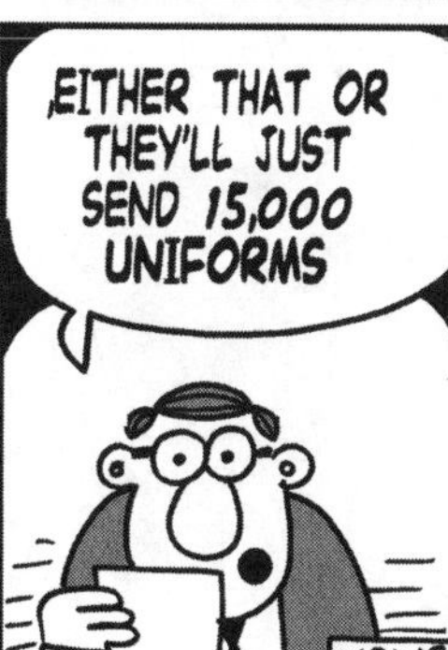

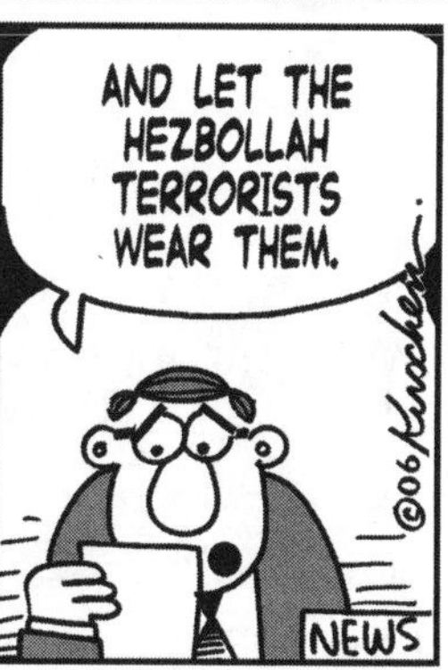

THOMAS "TAB" BOLDT, Calgary Sun

PETAR PISMETROVIC, Austria

THOMAS "TAB" BOLDT, Calgary Sun

CHRISTO
KOMARNITSKI
Bulgaria

JOHN TREVER, Albuquerque Journal

ARES
Cuba

JOHN DARKOW
Columbia Daily Tribune (MO)

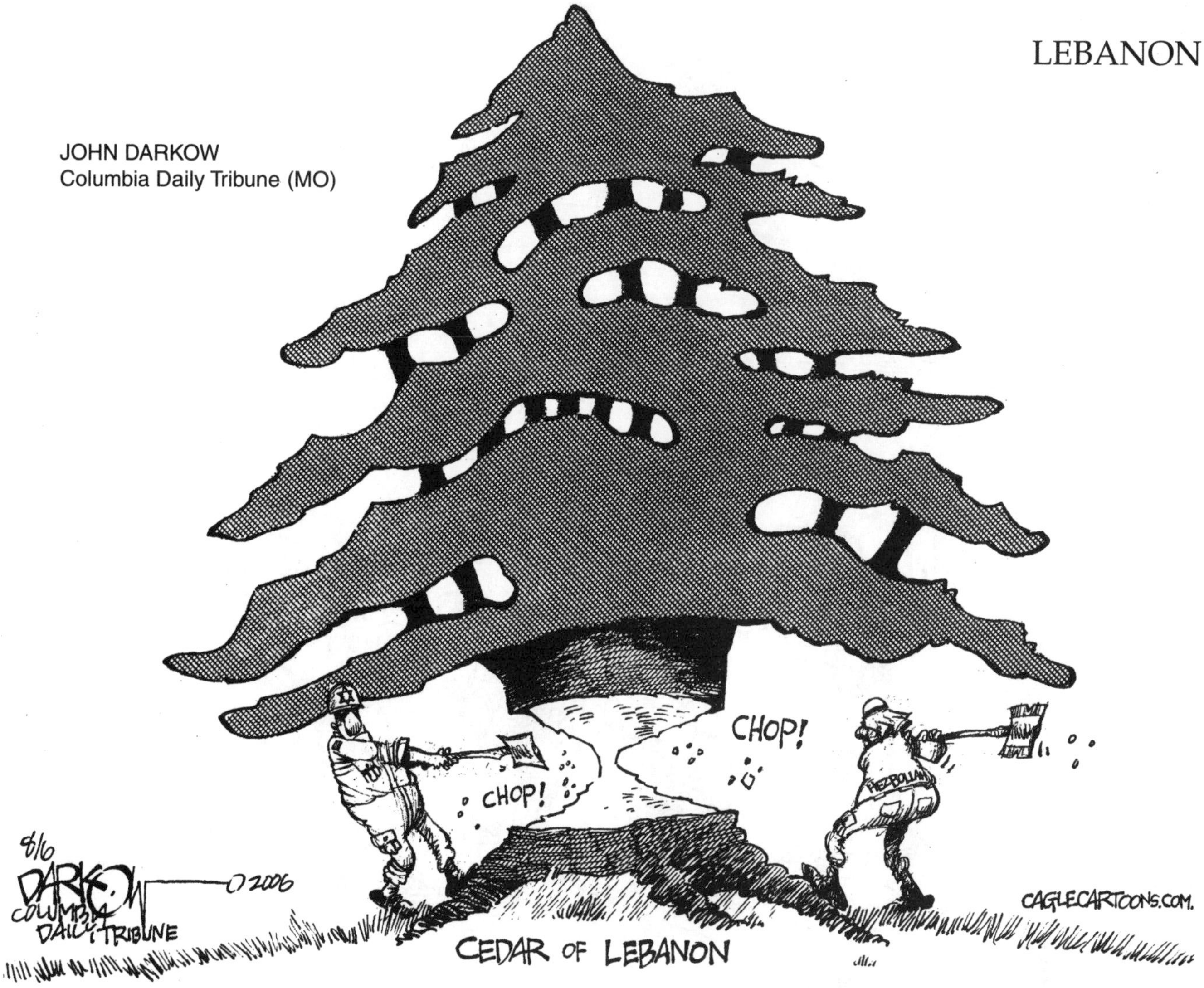
CHOP!
CHOP!
8/6
DARKOW ©2006
COLUMBIA DAILY TRIBUNE
CAGLECARTOONS.COM.
CEDAR OF LEBANON

FREDERICK DELIGNE
Nice-Matin
France

UN
LEBANON
DELIGNE

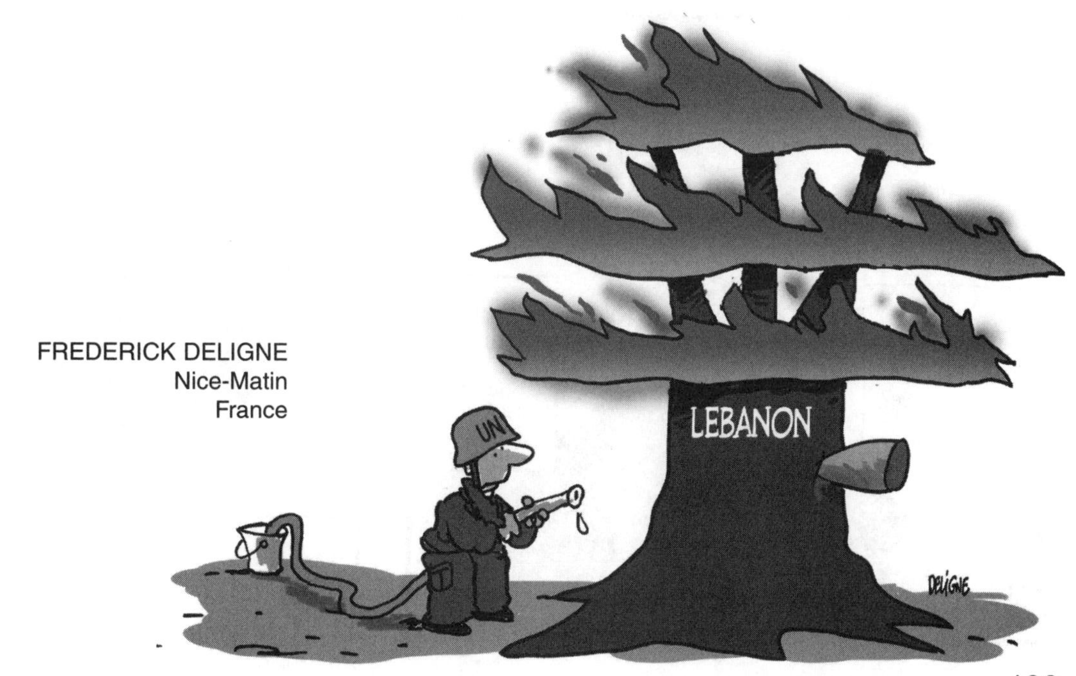

PETAR PISMETROVIC
Austria

GUY BADEAUX, Journal LeDroit, Canada

THOMAS "TAB" BOLDT
Calgary Sun

GUY BADEAUX, Journal LeDroit, Canada

JULIUS JENS HANSEN, Denmark

Mobile Hezbollahn rocket-launcher.

ROBERT ARIAIL
The State, (SC)

OLLE JOHANSSON, Sweden

PATRICK CHAPPATTE, International Herald Tribune

KIRK ANDERSON

PETAR PISMETROVIC
Austria

HALF SOCIAL SERVICES, HALF TERRORISM... NOBODY CAN SAY WE'RE DISPROPORTIONATE!

HEZBOLLAH DAYCARE and ROCKET CENTER

JOHN TREVER
Albuquerque
Journal

GUY BADEAUX, Journal LeDroit, Canada

MALCOLM EVANS
New Zealand

KIRK
WALTERS
Toledo Blade

KEN CATALINO

GUY BADEAUX, Journal LeDroit, Canada

OSMANI
SIMANCA
Brazil
www.caglecartoons.com/espanol

MIKE LANE, Cagle Cartoons

JACK OHMAN, Portland Oregonian

MICHAEL KOUNTOURIS
Greece

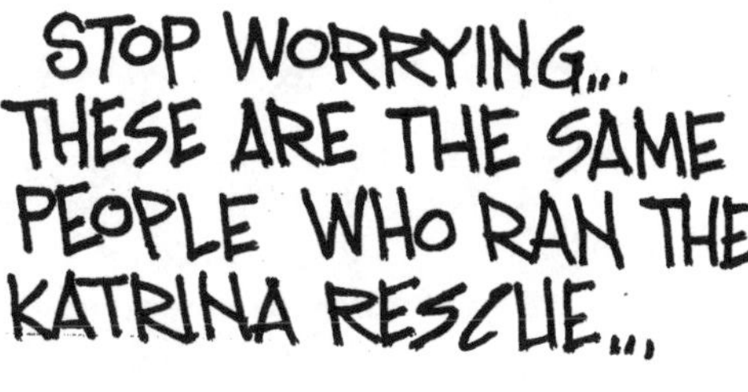

BILL SCHORR

MIKE LESTER, Rome News Tribune (GA)

ED STEIN, Rocky Mountain News

ALEN LAUZAN, Chile
(opposite page)

DARYL CAGLE
MSNBC.COM
(right)

USA
HEZBOLLAH
IRAN
DARYL CAGLE
MSNBC.COM

WALT HANDELSMAN, Newsday

DAN WASSERMAN, Boston Globe

Iran Nukes

Iran continued on its defiant pursuit of nuclear technology this year amidst demands from President Bush and the U.N. Security Council. Iranian President, Ahmadinejad, gave fiery speeches, promising to erase Israel from the map, and denying the Holocaust. As the world debated what to do about Iran's nukes, many cartoonists speculated on when the Bush administration would set its sights on Iran as a sequel to Iraq.

RAINER HACHFELD
Germany

STEVE SACK, Minneapolis Star-Tribune

BRIAN FAIRRINGTON
Cagle Cartoons

R.J. MATSON, St. Louis Post Dispatch

WAYNE STAYSKAL

DAN WASSERMAN, Boston Globe

DICK LOCHER, Chicago Tribune

MIKE LESTER, Rome News Tribune (GA)

WALT HANDELSMAN, Newsday

PATRICK CHAPPATTE
International Herald Tribune

DARYL CAGLE, MSNBC.com
(left and bottom left)

ARES
Cuba

R.J. MATSON
St. Louis
Post Dispatch

JOHN DARKOW
Columbia Daily Tribune (MO)

ENAD HAJJAJ
Jordan

PAUL COMBS, Tampa Tribune

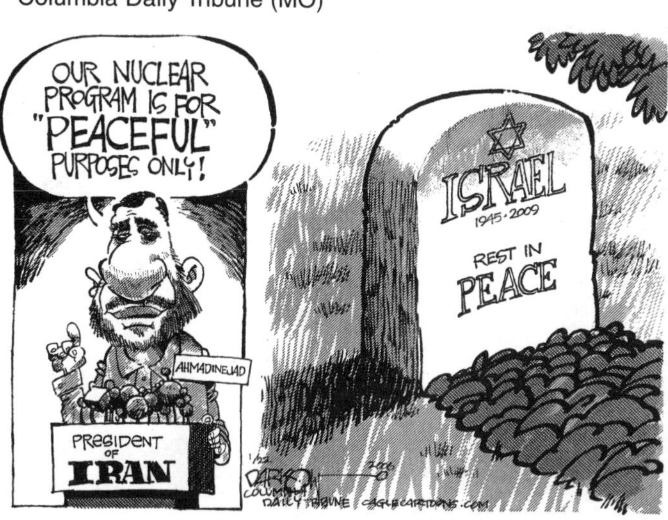

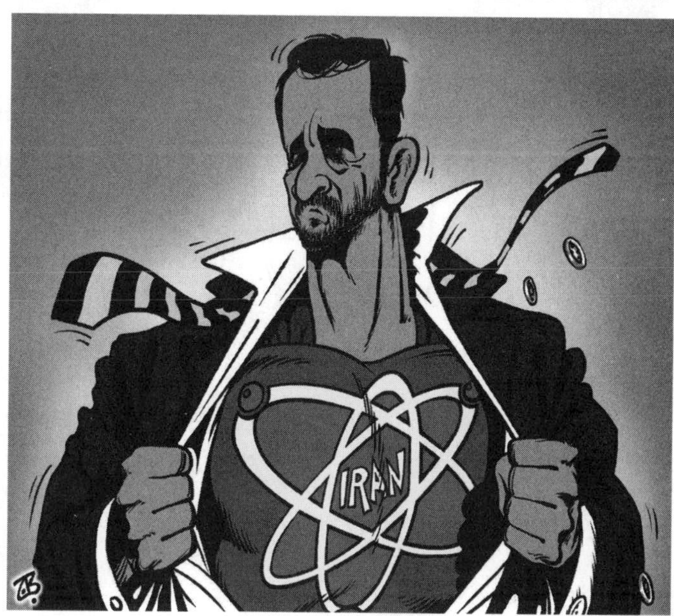

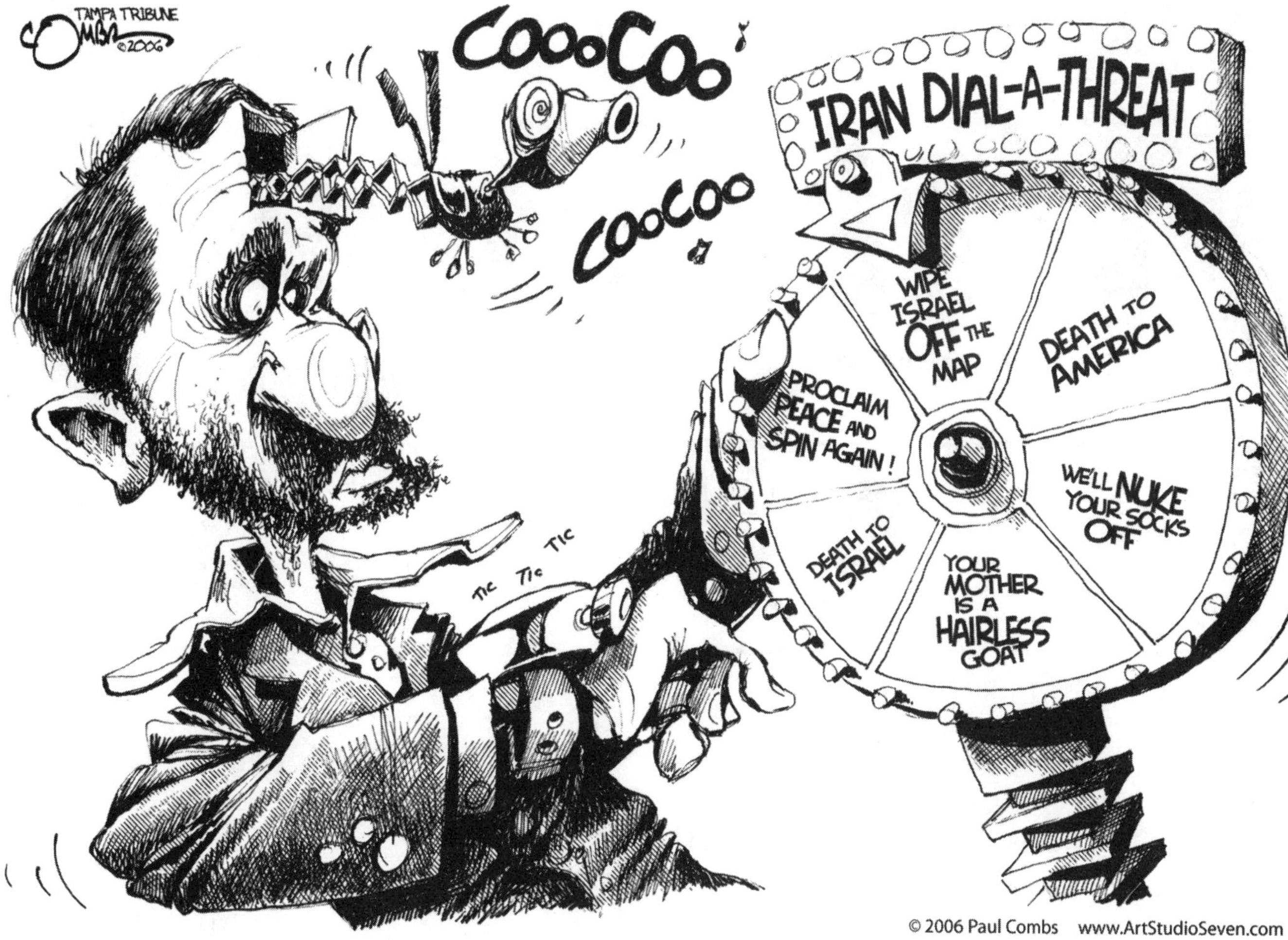

© 2006 Paul Combs www.ArtStudioSeven.com

BRIAN ADCOCK, Scotland

JERRY HOLBERT, Boston Herald

CAMERON CARDOW, Ottawa Citizen (Canada)

STEVE SACK, Minneapolis Star Tribune

MIKE LANE, Cagle Cartoons

ADAM ZYGLIS, Buffalo News

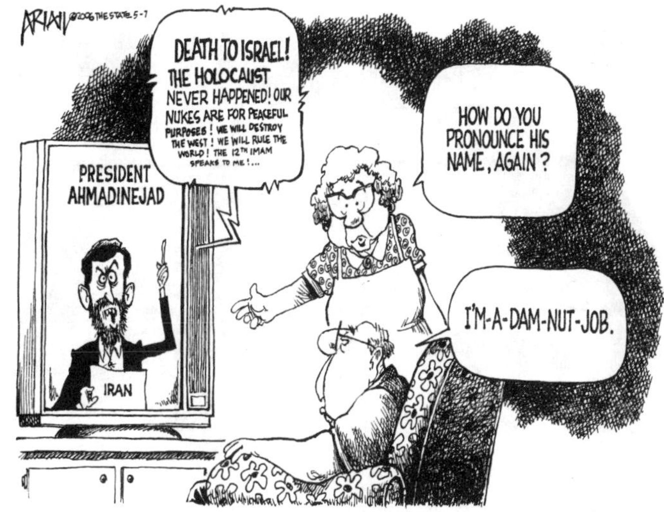

ROBERT ARIAIL, The State (SC)

ERIC ALLIE, Politicalcartoons.com

ERIC DEVERICKS
Seattle Times

ED STEIN
Rocky Mountain News

MIKE KEEFE, Denver Post

JEFF KOTERBA, Omaha World Herald

BRIAN FAIRRINGTON, Cagle Cartoons

CHUCK ASAY, Colorado Springs Gazette

DAVID FITZSIMMONS, Arizona Daily Star

PATRICK CHAPPATTE, International Herald Tribune

DWANE POWELL, Raliegh News & Observer

STEVE KELLEY, New Orleans Times Picayune

North Korea

Tensions between the U.S. and North Korea increased this year as North Korea's nutty leader Kim Jong Il detonated a nuclear bomb. North Korea had everyone nervous, including editorial cartoonists.

JEFF PARKER
Florida Today

MIKE THOMPSON
Detroit Free Press

MIKE LESTER
Rome News
Tribune (GA)

ELEVATOR SHOES

CORKY TRINIDAD, Honolulu Star Bulletin

JACK OHMAN, Portland Oregonian

PROJECTILE DYSFUNCTION

REX BABIN, Sacramento Bee

CHRIS BRITT, State Journal-Register (IL)

ANOTHER FAILED NORTH KOREAN WARHEAD TEST.

HENRY PAYNE, Detroit News

TO THE LAUNCH PAD

CAL GRONDAHL, Utah Standard Examiner

MIKE KEEFE, Denver Post

JOHN COLE, Scranton Times-Tribune

NATE BEELER, Washington Examiner

DICK LOCHER, Chicago Tribune

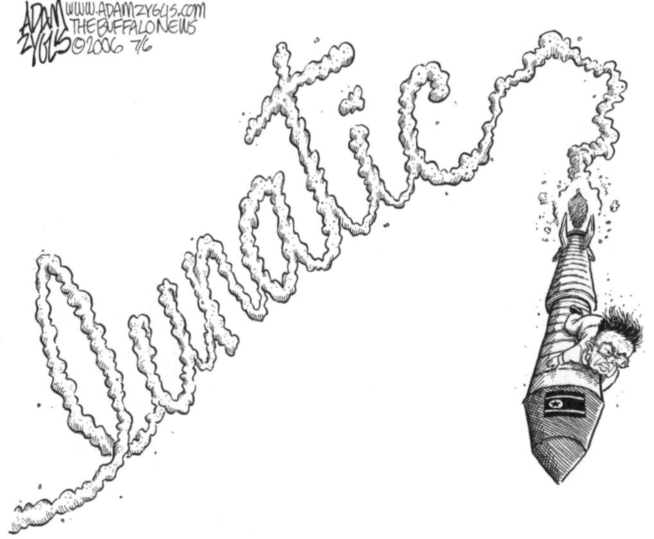

ADAM ZYGLIS, Buffalo News

DON WRIGHT, Palm Beach Post

R.P. OVERMYER
Hollywood Dog

NORTH-KOREAN-WEAPONS-OF-MASS-DESTRUCTION-ADVISOR BLAMES RECENT NUCLEAR EXPLOSION ON PESKY ROADRUNNER.

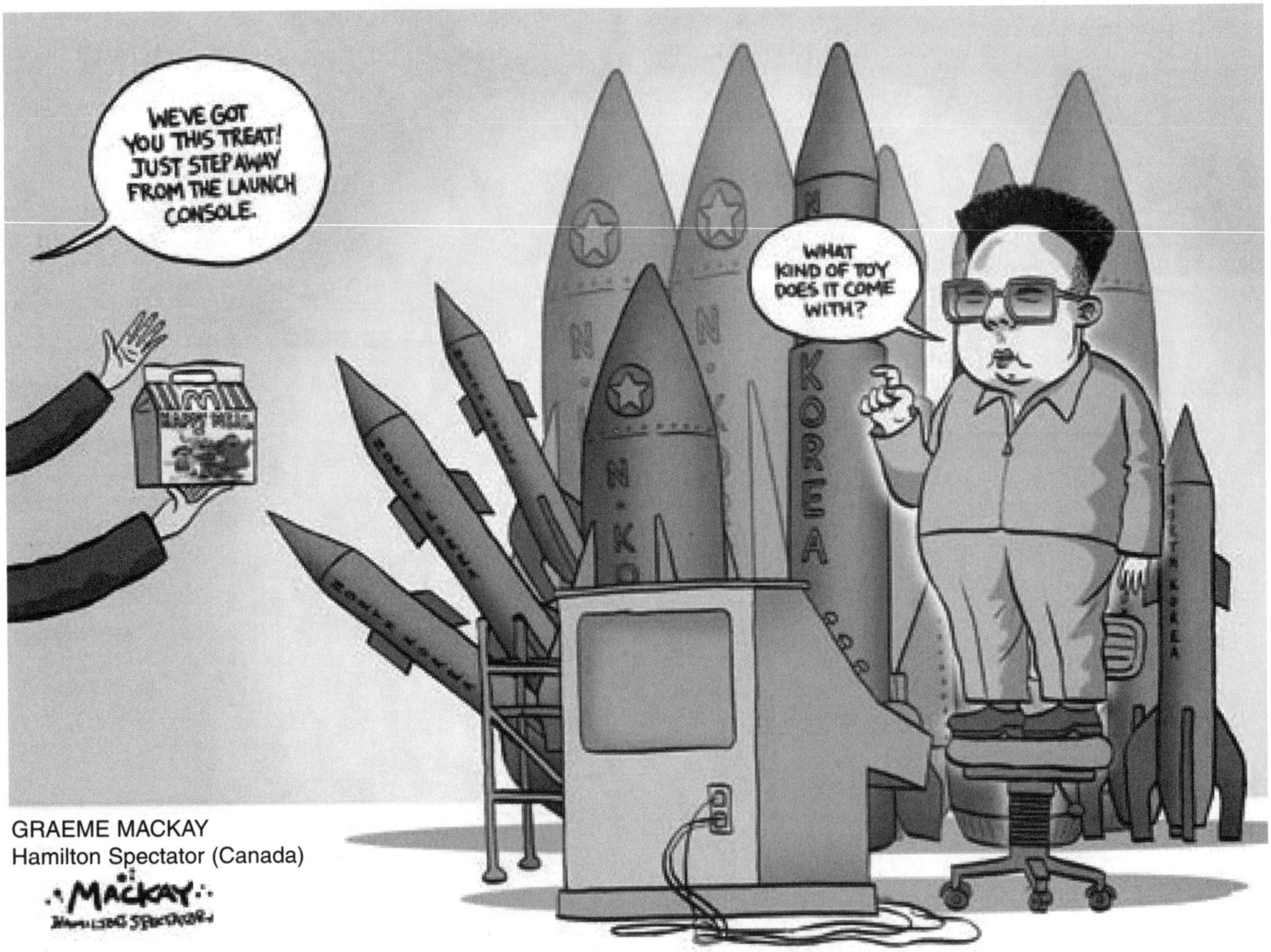

GRAEME MACKAY
Hamilton Spectator (Canada)

DARYL CAGLE
MSNBC.com

JIMMY MARGULIES, The Record (NJ)

DANA SUMMERS, Orlando Sentinel

DAVID HORSEY, Seattle Post Intelligencer (left)

DWANE POWELL, Raleigh News & Observer

DREW SHENEMAN, Newark Star Ledger

NICK ANDERSON
Houston Chronicle

BOB
GORRELL

BLINDED BY THE LIGHT

NORTH KOREA

RIBER HANSSON
Sweden

LARRY WRIGHT
Detroit News

JOHN TREVER, Albuquerque Journal (above)

BILL LEAK, The Australian, Sydney

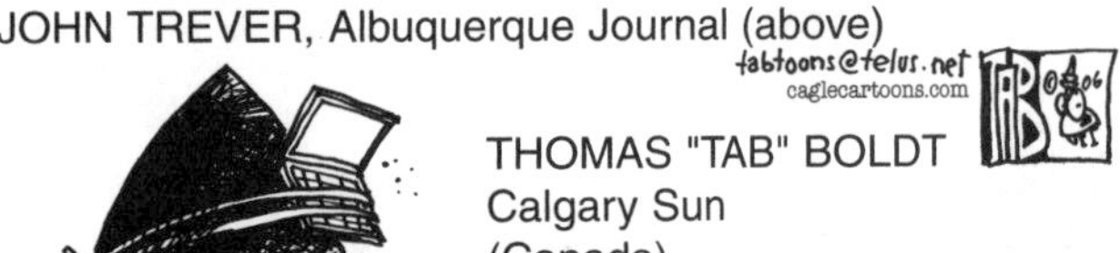

THOMAS "TAB" BOLDT
Calgary Sun
(Canada)

BILL LEAK, The Australian, Sydney

VINCE O'FARRELL, Illawarra Mercury, Australia (below)

KIRK WALTERS
Toledo Blade

STEVE BREEN, San Diego Union Tribune

STEVE SACK
Minneapolis
Star Tribune

JOHN DEERING, Arkansas Democrat Gazette

PATRICK CORRIGAN, Toronto Star

ANGEL
BOLIGAN
El Universal
Mexico

Iraq—Five Years Later

The war in Iraq continued in 2006, with no end in sight. American public support continued on a downward spiral as President Bush insisted that he would "stay the course." Cartoonists reflected spreading pessimism.

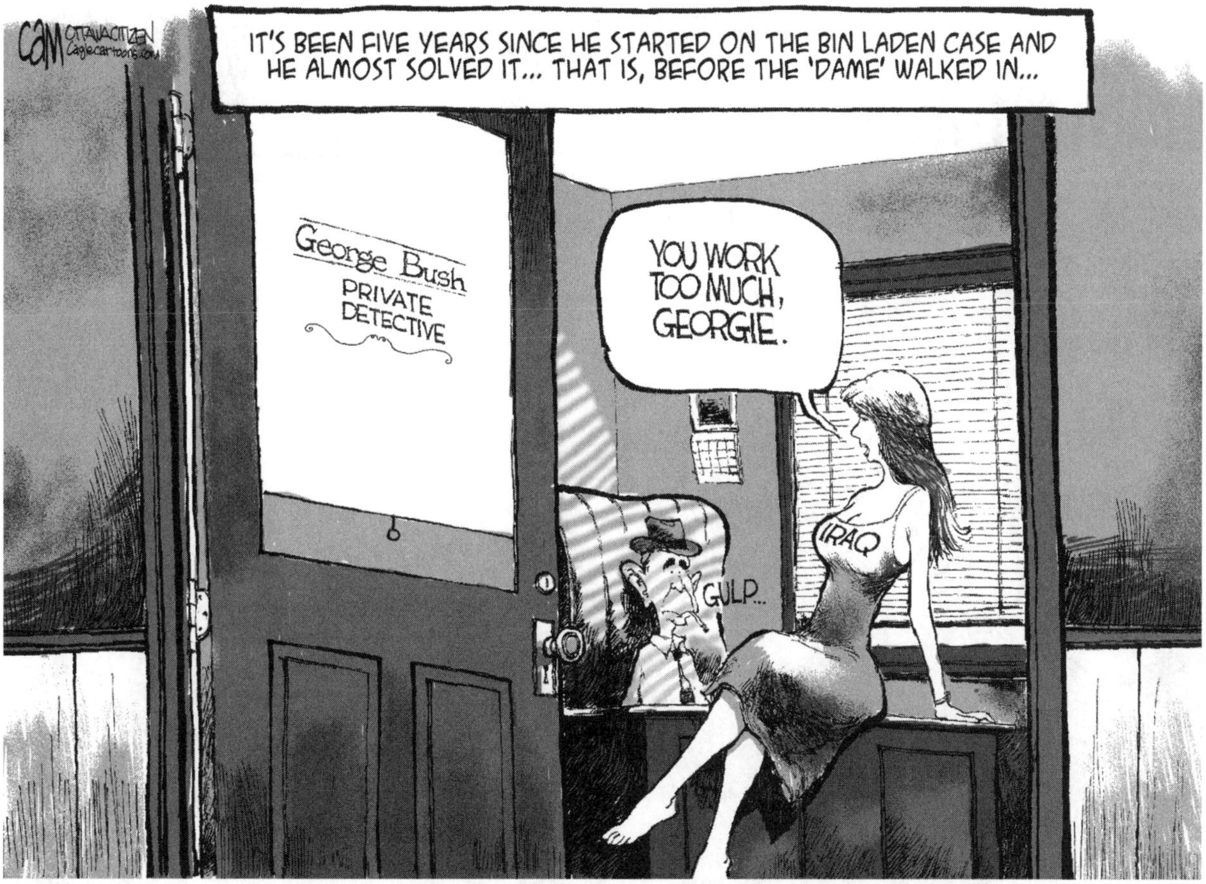
CAM OTTAWA CITIZEN Caglecartoons.com
IT'S BEEN FIVE YEARS SINCE HE STARTED ON THE BIN LADEN CASE AND HE ALMOST SOLVED IT... THAT IS, BEFORE THE 'DAME' WALKED IN...
George Bush
PRIVATE DETECTIVE
YOU WORK TOO MUCH, GEORGIE.
IRAQ
GULP...

CAMERON CARDOW
Ottawa Citizen (Canada)

COST OF IRAQ WAR
300,000,000,000
YOUR SHARE
1,250
SINGER

ANDY SINGER, No Exit

EDUCATION
HEALTH CARE
ENVIRONMENT
SOCIAL & EMERGENCY SERVICES
TAX CUTS FOR RICH
IRAQ WAR
SINGER
$ 1.7 TRILLION
$300 BILLION SO FAR

ANDY SINGER, No Exit

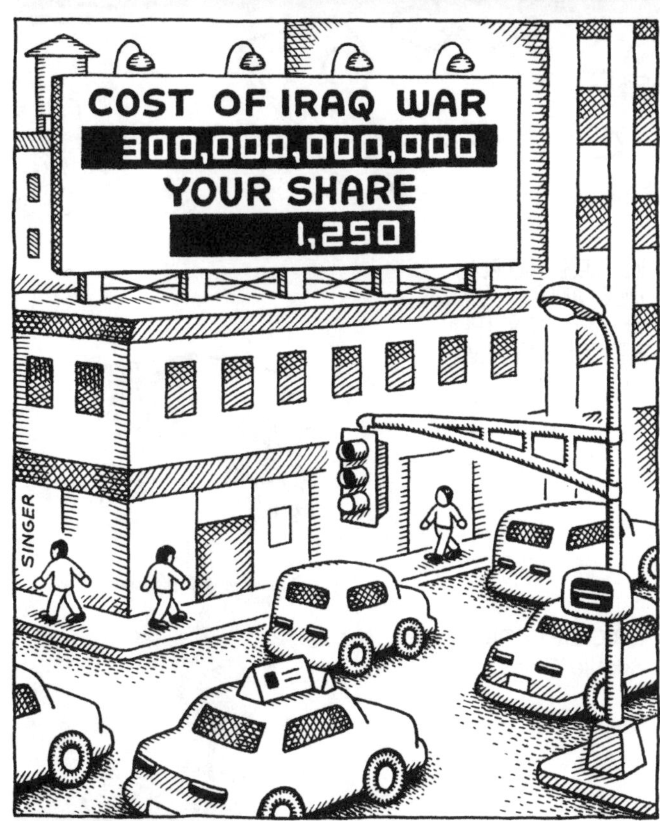

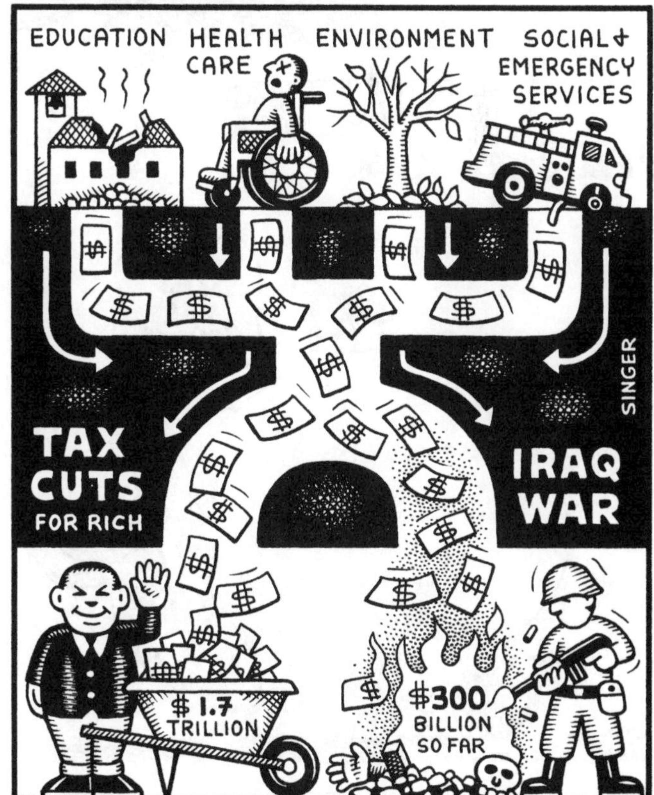

JERRY HOLBERT
Boston Herald

ETTA HULME, Ft. Worth Star Telegram

ERIC DEVERICKS
Seattle Times

MATT DAVIES
Journal News (NY)

VINCE O'FARRELL, Illawarra Mercury, Australia

JOHN DEERING, Arkansas Democrat Gazette

BRUCE BEATTIE, Daytona News-Journal

MIKE LANE, Cagle Cartoons

JIM DAY, Las Vegas Review-Journal

DON WRIGHT, Palm Beach Post

JIMMY MARGULIES, The Record (NJ)

KIRK ANDERSON

IRAQ'S IMPROVING INFRASTRUCTURE

KIRK ANDERSON

HOW COME JOURNALISTS DON'T SHOW US ALL THE GOOD THINGS HAPPENING IN IRAQ?

PETER NICHOLSON, The Australian, Sydney

MICHAEL RAMIREZ, Investors Business Daily

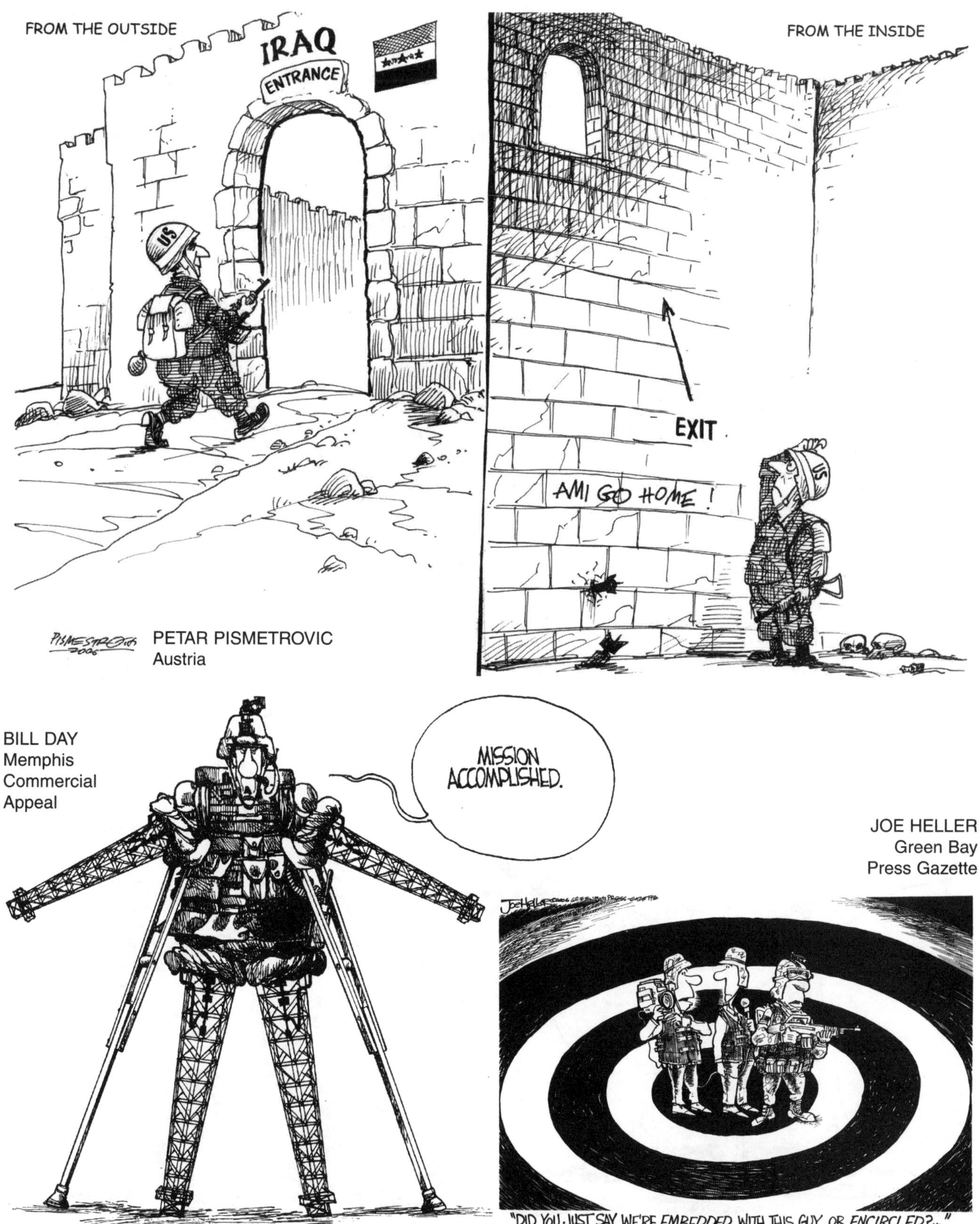

PETAR PISMETROVIC
Austria

BILL DAY
Memphis
Commercial
Appeal

JOE HELLER
Green Bay
Press Gazette

STEVE SACK
Minneapolis Star Tribune

MIKE LANE, Cagle Cartoons

ED STEIN, Rocky Mountain News

DARYL CAGLE
MSNBC.com

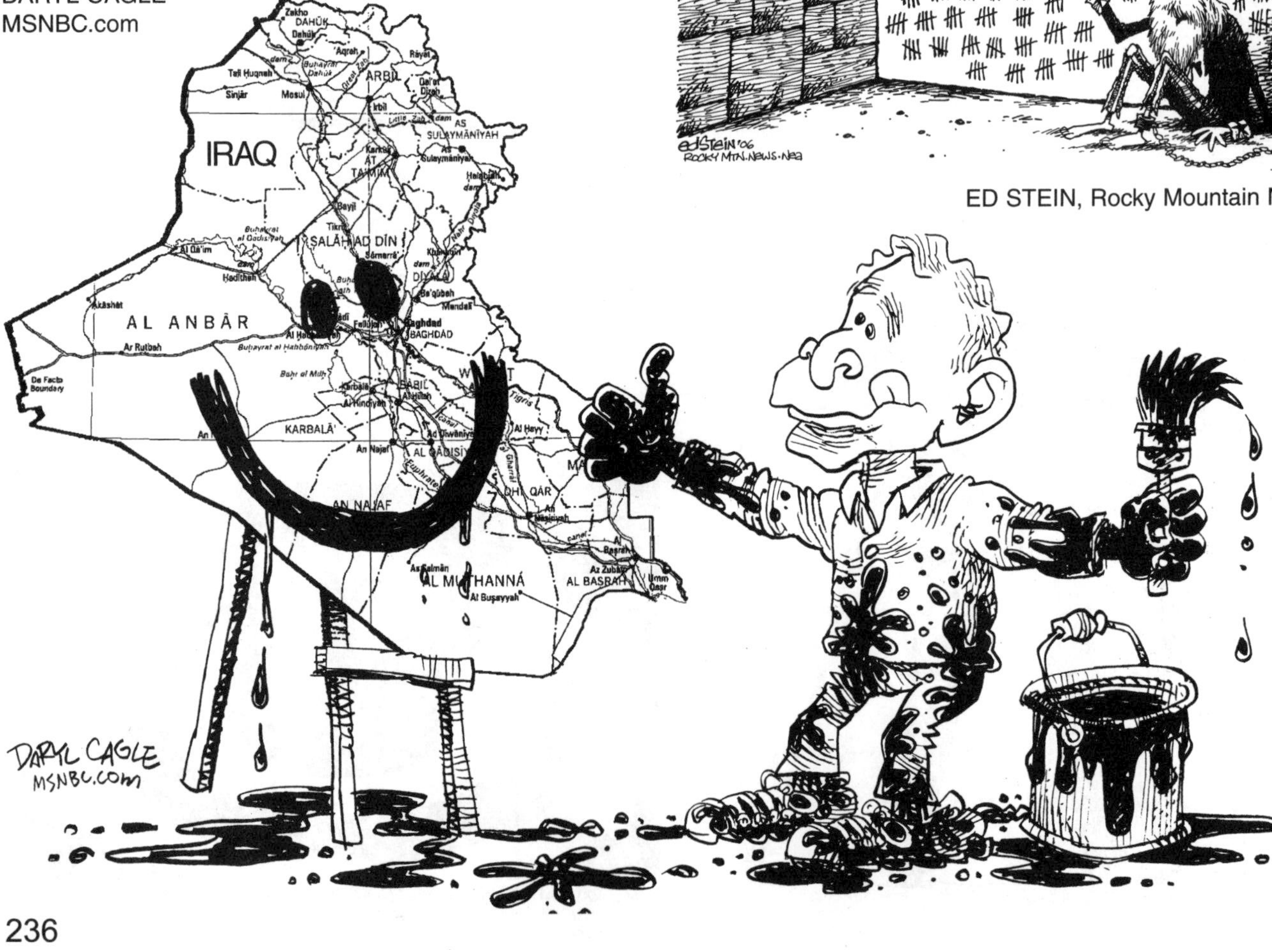

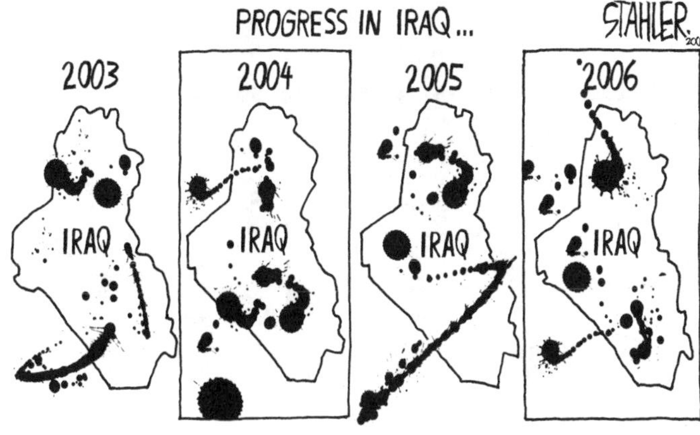

JEFF STAHLER, Columbus Dispatch

VIC HARVILLE, Stephens Media Group

JOHN TREVER, Albuquerque Journal

JOHN BRANCH, San Antonio Express News

PATRICK O'CONNOR, Los Angeles Daily News

INGRID RICE, British Columbia, Canada

BOB ENGLEHART, Hartford Courant

MIKE KEEFE, Denver Post

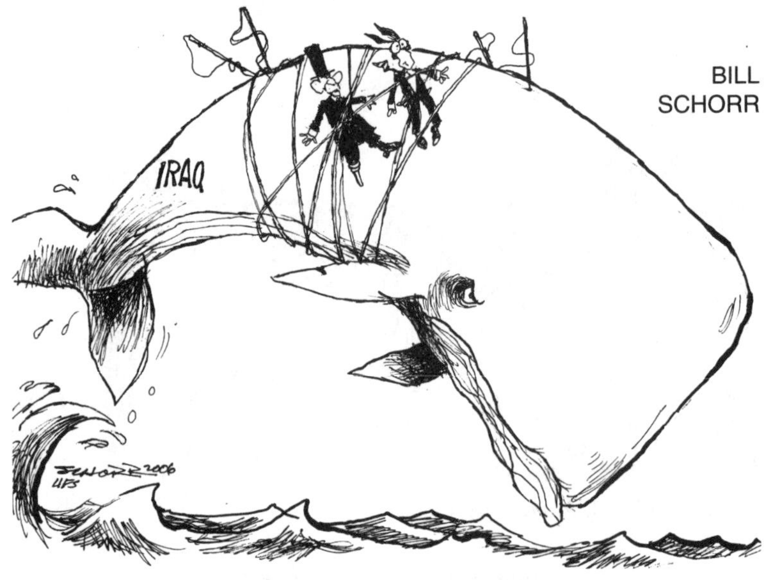

BILL SCHORR

JEFF PARKER, Florida Today

IRAQ

"I'M THE ROWER AND WHEREVER I ROW IS RIGHT."

PAT BAGLEY
Salt Lake Tribune
(UT)

PAUL COMBS
Tampa Tribune

Haditha

After a U.S. Marine was killed in the Iraqi city of Haditha, a dozen Marines from the same unit allegedly exacted revenge on the town, murdering 24 Iraqis, including 11 women and children. Following an investigation, the U.S. military found probable cause for charging the Marines. Cartoonists drew parallels between the Haditha killings and the My Lai massacre in Vietnam.

NICK ANDERSON, Houston Chronicle

WALT HANDELSMAN
Newsday

STEVE BENSON, Arizona Republic

SCOTT STANTIS, Birmingham News

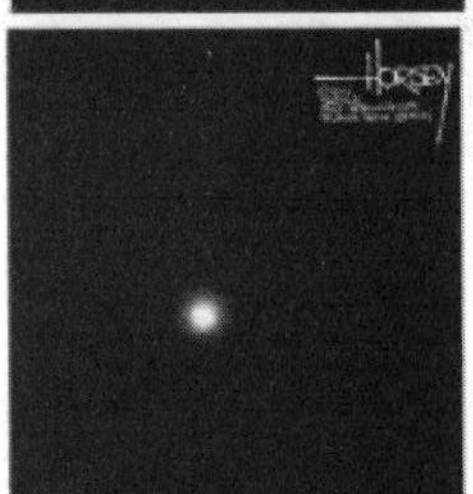

DAVID HORSEY
Seattle Post
Intelligencer

ED STEIN, Rocky Mountain News

EMAD HAJJAJ
Jordan

HADITHA

R.J. MATSON
St. Louis
Post Dispatch

CLAY JONES, Freelance Star (VA)

ROB ROGERS, Pittsburgh Post Gazette

CHIP BOK, Akron Beacon Journal

BRUCE BEATTIE, Daytona News Journal

Liquid Terror

The international traveling community was riled again this year. Over the summer, officials in London discovered a terrorist plot to detonate bombs aboard U.S.-bound planes—bombs made from liquid explosives and disguised as sports drinks. Though the plan was not close to being implemented, the FAA temporarily banned all liquids and gels from being carried aboard, from Chapstick to perfume to bottled water, even if it was purchased inside the airport. Many cartoonists empathized with the thirsty, inconvenienced travelers worldwide.

NICK ANDERSON
Houston Chronicle

ROB ROGERS
Pittsburgh
Post Gazette

JOHN DARKOW
Columbia Daily
Tribune (MO)

PATRICK CORRIGAN
Toronto Star

MALCOLM EVANS
New Zealand

JOE HELLER
Green Bay Press-Gazette

JACK OHMAN
Portland Oregonian

OHMAN THE OREGONIAN © 2006 · TRIBUNE MEDIA SERVICES · 8/11

ANOTHER BRAVE SOLDIER IN THE WAR ON TERROR...

Security

Chanel N° 5

Harrods LONDON

VERSACE

TRA

CHAN LOWE, South Florida Sun Sentinel

CHIP BOK, Akron Beacon Journal

DON WRIGHT, Palm Beach Post

MARK STREETER, Savannah Morning News

BILL DAY, Memphis Commercial Appeal

J.D. CROWE, Mobile Register

MATT DAVIES, Journal News (NY)

KIRK WALTERS, Toledo Blade

CHRIS BRITT, State Journal Register (IL)

YAAKOV KIRSCHEN
Dry Bones, Jerusalem Post

MIKE LESTER
Rome News Tribune (GA)

LARRY WRIGHT
Detroit News

MICHAEL RAMIREZ
Investors Business Daily

JEFF STAHLER
Columbus Dispatch

STEVE NEASE
Oakville Beaver (Canada)

JOHN DEERING, Arkansas Democrat Gazette

FREDERICK DELIGNE, Nice-Matin, France

STEVE BREEN
San Diego
Union Tribune

CHUCK ASAY
Colorado Springs Gazette

tabtoons@telus.net
caglecartoons.com
TERROR
THE WEST

Nightmare at 30,000 Feet

THOMAS "TAB" BOLDT
Calgary Sun
(Canada)

STEVE KELLEY
New Orleans Times Picayune

MATT BORS
Idiot Box

THANKS. ENJOY YOUR OVERBOOKED FLIGHT!

CAMERON CARDOW, Ottawa Citizen (Canada)

STEVE BENSON, Arizona Republic

Guantanamo

The U.S. Guantanamo or GITMO prison camp in Cuba drew strong criticism and allegations of torture from both Americans and the international community. Gitmo prisoners were classified as "enemy combatants" and detained without trial; the U.S. administration claimed that under that definition, the prisoners weren't entitled to protection under the Geneva Convention. This year the Supreme Court struck down this interpretation, reinstating Geneva rights to all prisoners of the war on terror. Guantanamo cartoons were popular this year, as hooded prisoners became symbols for the Bush administration's brutality—or, as more conservative cartoonists portrayed them, as the contained evil of terrorism.

JOHN TREVER, Albuquerque Journal

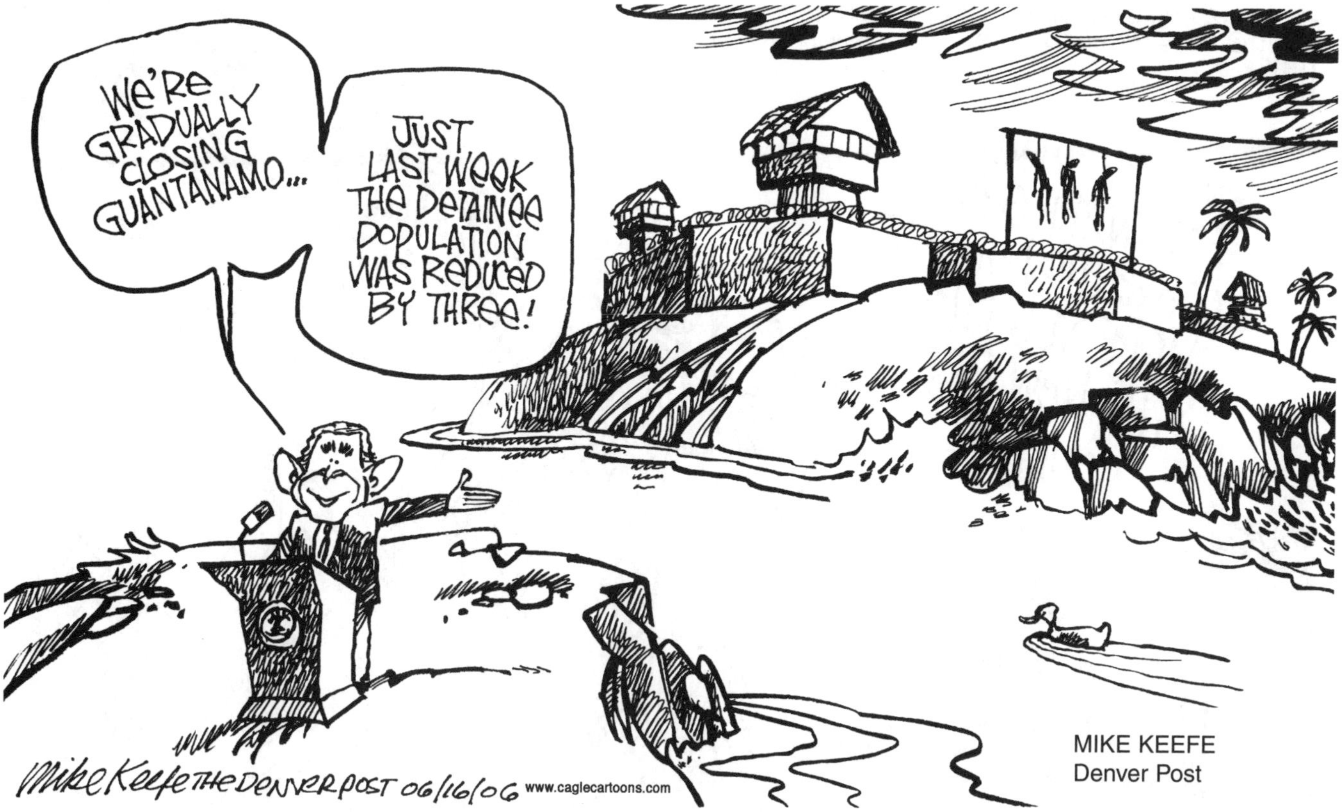
WE'RE GRADUALLY CLOSING GUANTANAMO...
JUST LAST WEEK THE DETAINEE POPULATION WAS REDUCED BY THREE!
MIKE KEEFE THE DENVER POST 06/16/06
www.caglecartoons.com

MIKE KEEFE
Denver Post

ADAM ZYGLIS, Buffalo News

THIS PLACE IS DESTROYING THE MORAL INTEGRITY OF AMERICA...
WE HAVE TO SHUT IT DOWN!
'GITMO' 3 SUICIDES
Wedding Chapel
GAYS WELCOME!

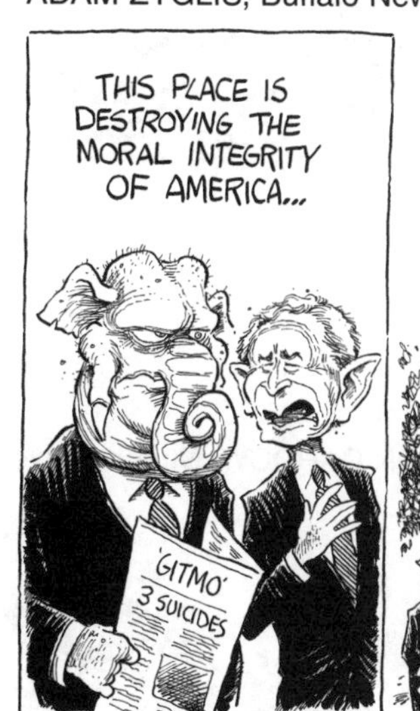

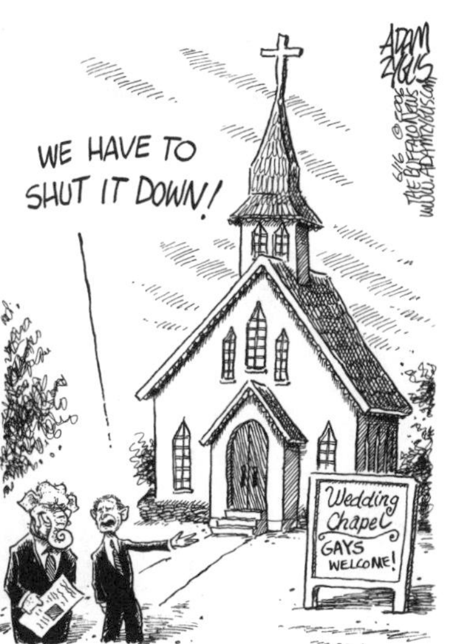

JACK OHMAN, Portland Oregonian

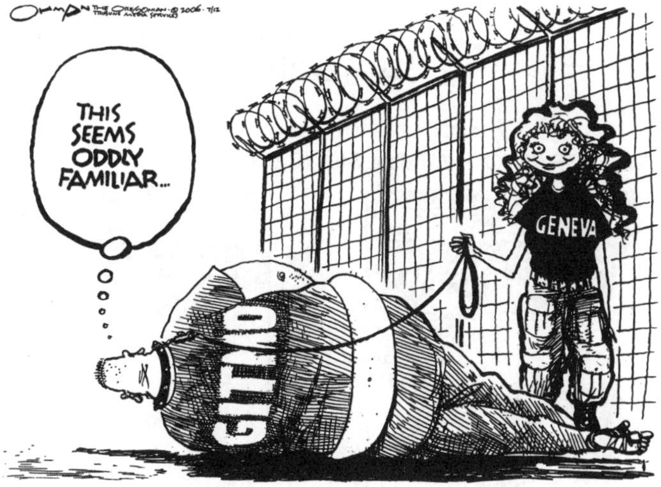
THIS SEEMS ODDLY FAMILIAR...
GENEVA
GITMO

JIMMY MARGULIES, The Record (NJ)

Sure...we'd like to shut down Guantanamo...
...but we can't simply release the detainees...
...and return them to the newspapers they write for...
MARGULIES

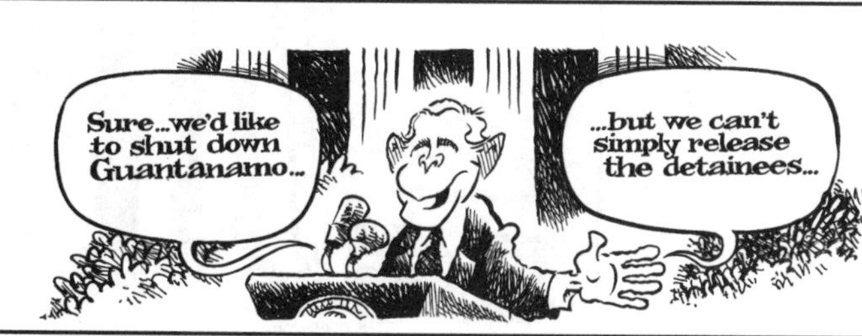

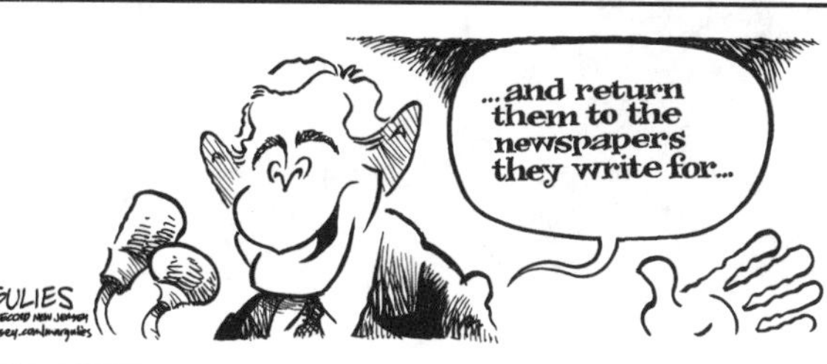

PLANTE THE CHATTANOOGA TIMES 7·11·2006 ©2006-BRUCE@PLANTEINK.COM

BRUCE PLANTE
Chattanooga Times Free Press

GUANTANAMO

=MUMBLE, MUMBLE= FOLLOW THE GENEVA CONVENTION =HMMPF= HOPE YOU LIKE THE NEW BED SHEETS!

MIKE GRASTON, Windsor Star (Canada)

CAMERON CARDOW, Ottawa Citizen

CHRISTO KOMARNITSKI, Bulgaria

CORKY TRINIDAD, Honolulu Star Bulletin

KIRK ANDERSON

Memorial Cartoons

Memorial cartoons provide cartoonists with the rare opportunity to praise or condemn the lives of notable public figures. Coretta Scott King, Dana Reeve, Don Knotts and "Crocodile Hunter" Steve Irwin were just some of the esteemed celebrities we lost this year. We also have some new candidates for Hell, including Al Qaeda kingpin Abu Musab Al Zarqawi, Serbia's ethnic cleanser, Slobodan Milosovic, and Enron's greedy Ken Lay.

SCOTT STANTIS, Birmingham News

JEFF STAHLER
Columbus Dispatch

BILL DAY, Memphis Commercial-Appeal

MARSHALL RAMSEY, Clarion Ledger (MI)

DANA REEVE
1961-2006

caglecartoons.com

©3/9/06 HARTFORD COURANT.

BOB ENGLEHART
Hartford Courant

MIKE LESTER
Rome News-Tribune
(GA)

RICHARD CROWSON, Witchita Eagle

SCOTT STANTIS
Birmingham News

...AND YET BARNEY FIFE'S LEGACY LIVES ON...

DARYL CAGLE
MSNBC.com

PETER NICHOLSON
The Australian,
Sydney

PAUL ZANETTI
Australia

DANA SUMMERS, Orlando Sentinel

GARY MARKSTEIN

BILL DAY
Memphis Commercial-Appeal

JUSTIN BILICKI

VINCE O'FARRELL
Illawarra Mercury
Australia

BROOKINS RICHMOND TIMES-DISPATCH 9/06
STEVE IRWIN ·1962-2006· CONSERVATIONIST

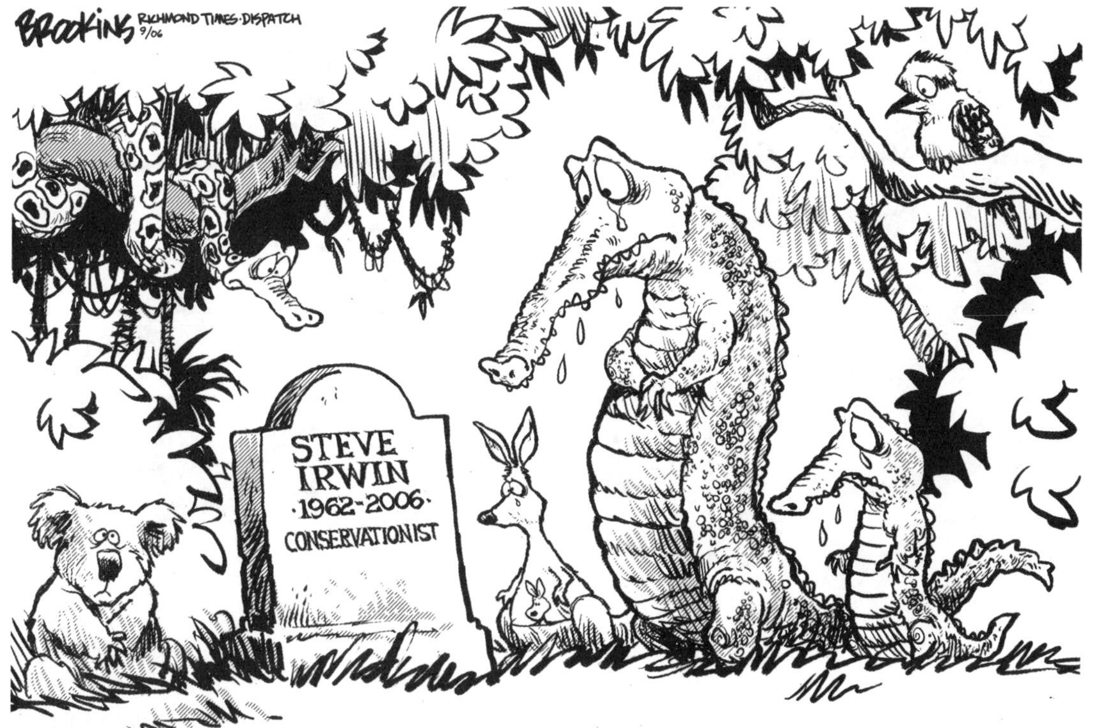

GARY BROOKINS
Raleigh News-Observer

REAL CROCODILE TEARS

WALT HANDELSMAN, Newsday

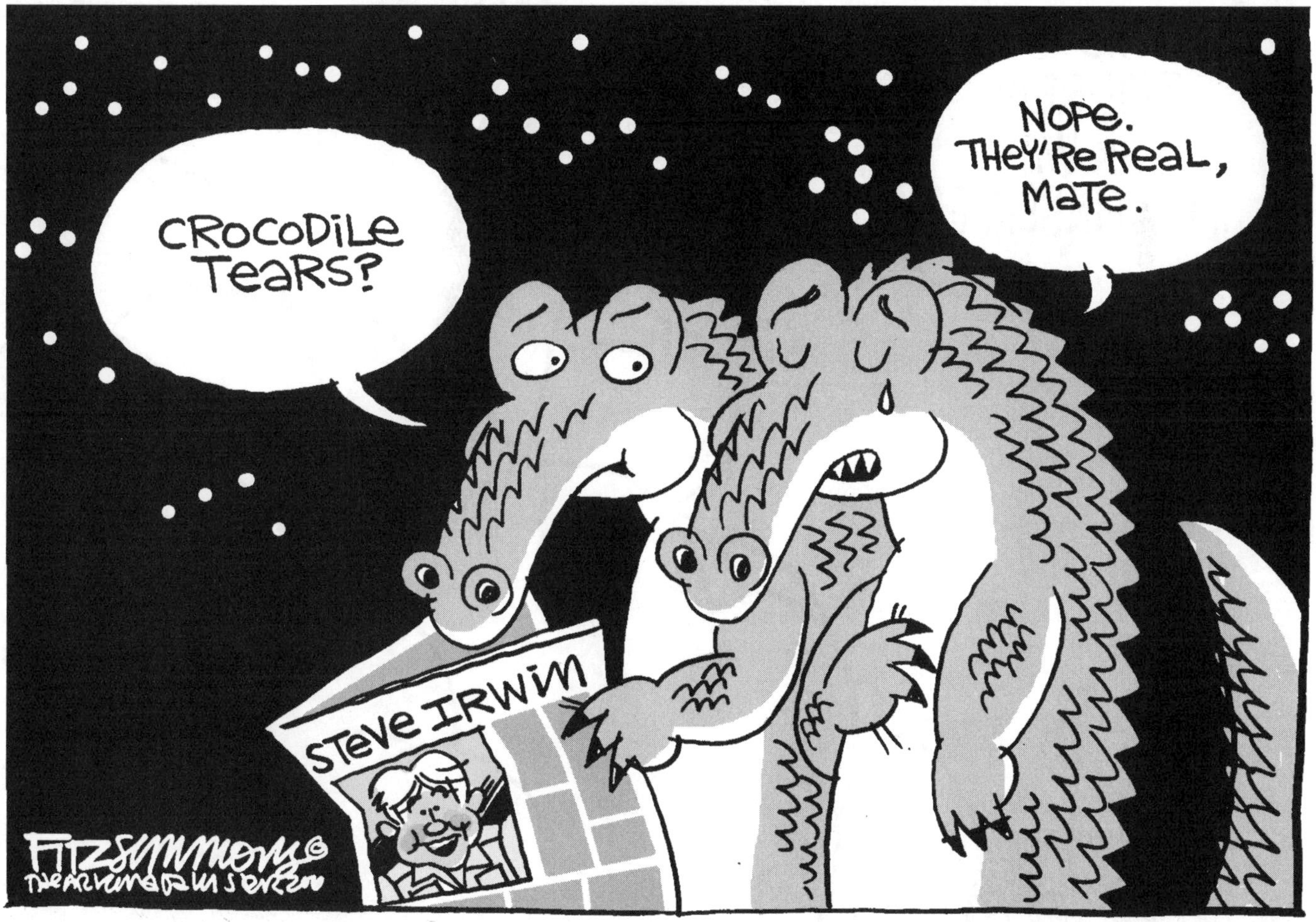
CROCODILE TEARS?
NOPE. THEY'RE REAL, MATE.
STEVE IRWIN
FITZSIMMONS ©

BOB ENGLEHART, Hartford Courant

CAMERON CARDOW, Ottawa Citizen

JEFF STAHLER
Columbus Dispatch

STAHLER
©THE COLUMBUS DISPATCH 2006

THIS IS THE REAL STAR WARS, MR. WEINBERGER.

MARK STREETER
Savannah Morning News

STEVE SACK
Minneapolis Star Tribune

WILSON PICKETT
1941-2006

SALLY

www.caglecartoons.com Mike Keefe THE DENVER POST 01/21/06

MIKE KEEFE
Denver Post

I'D LIKE TO REMEMBER KEN LAY... WHAT CAN I GET FOR A QUARTER?

FLOWERS

ENRON RETIREE

ROSES

MikeLane

MIKE LANE
Cagle Cartoons

BOB ENGLEHART
Hartford Courant

JOE HELLER
Green Bay
Press-Gazette

DANA
SUMMERS
Orlando
Sentinel

STEVE SACK, Minneapolis Star Tribune

JOHN BRANCH, San Antonio Express-News

JOHN COLE, Scranton Times-Tribune

M.e. COHEN
Politicalcartoons.com

MILOSEVIC

He DIED OF A NO HEART ATTACK.

. Cohen/HumorInk.com 03.12

RANDY BISH, Pittsburgh Tribune-Review

STEVE BREEN, San Diego Union Tribune

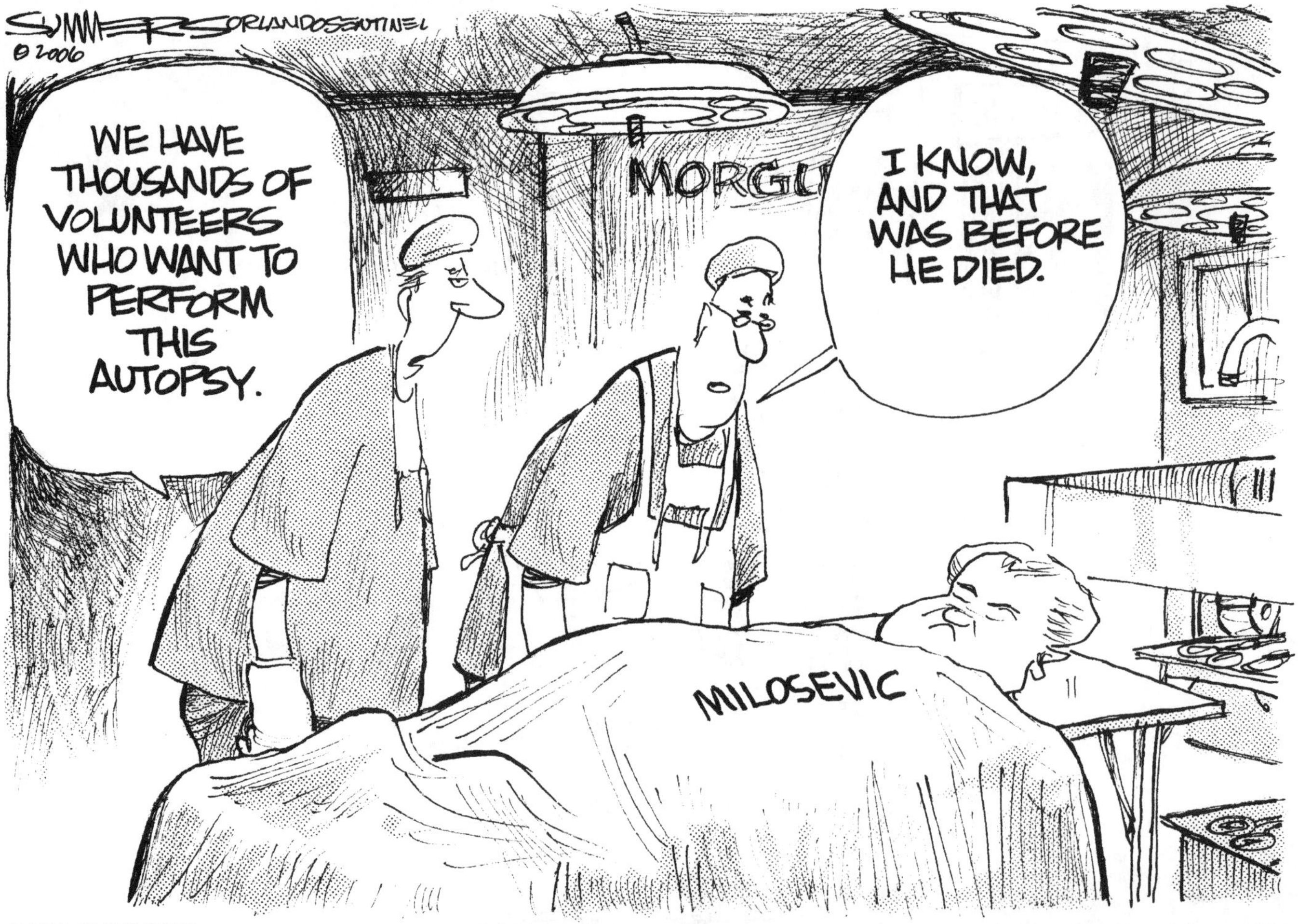
SUMMERS ORLANDO SENTINEL
© 2006
WE HAVE THOUSANDS OF VOLUNTEERS WHO WANT TO PERFORM THIS AUTOPSY.
I KNOW, AND THAT WAS BEFORE HE DIED.
MORGU
MILOSEVIC

DANA SUMMERS
Orlando Sentinel

STAR TRIBUNE SACK
MILOSOVIC FAN CLUB
MILOSOVIC FAN CLUB
MILOSOVIC FAN CLUB
AUTOGRAPHS

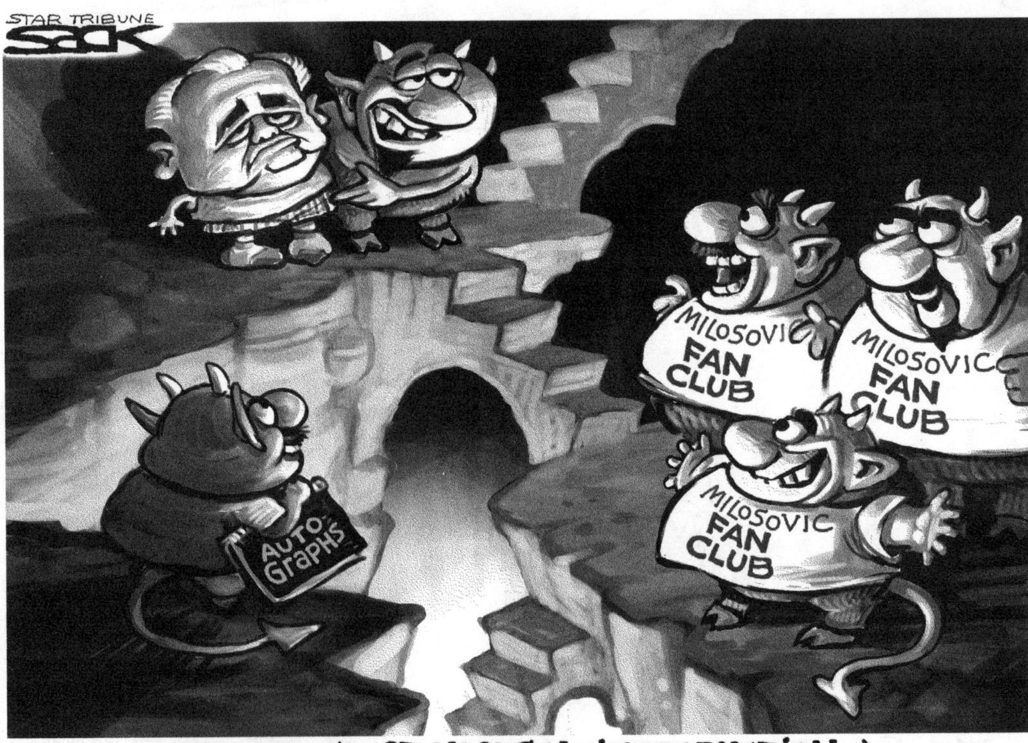

'OUR NEXT GUEST NEEDS NO INTRODUCTION....'

STEVE SACK
Minneapolis Star-Tribune

CAMERON CARDOW
Ottawa Citizen

JOHN SHERFFIUS
Boulder Daily Camera

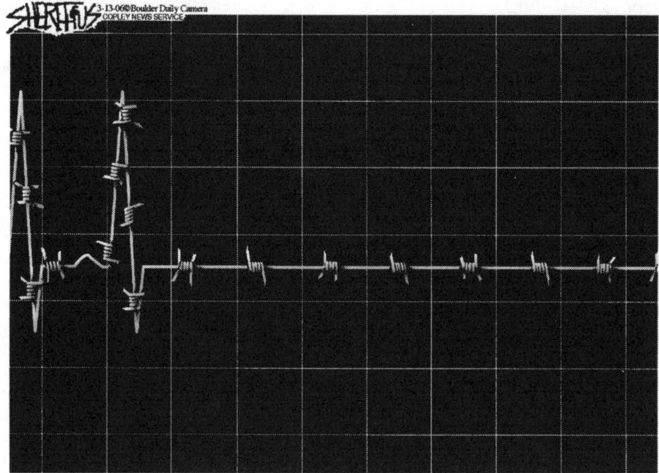

Milosevic's failed heart

PAT BAGLEY
Salt Lake Tribune (UT)

JOHN TREVER, Albuquerque Journal

STEVE KELLEY, New Orleans Times-Picayune

PAUL COMBS, Tampa Tribune

JUSTIN BILICKI

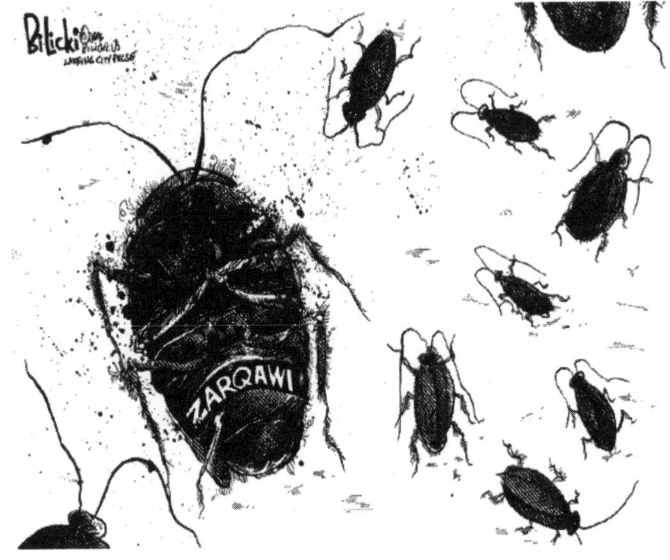

JEFF STAHLER, Columbus Dispatch

KEN CATALINO

CHRISTO
KOMARNITSKI
Bulgaria

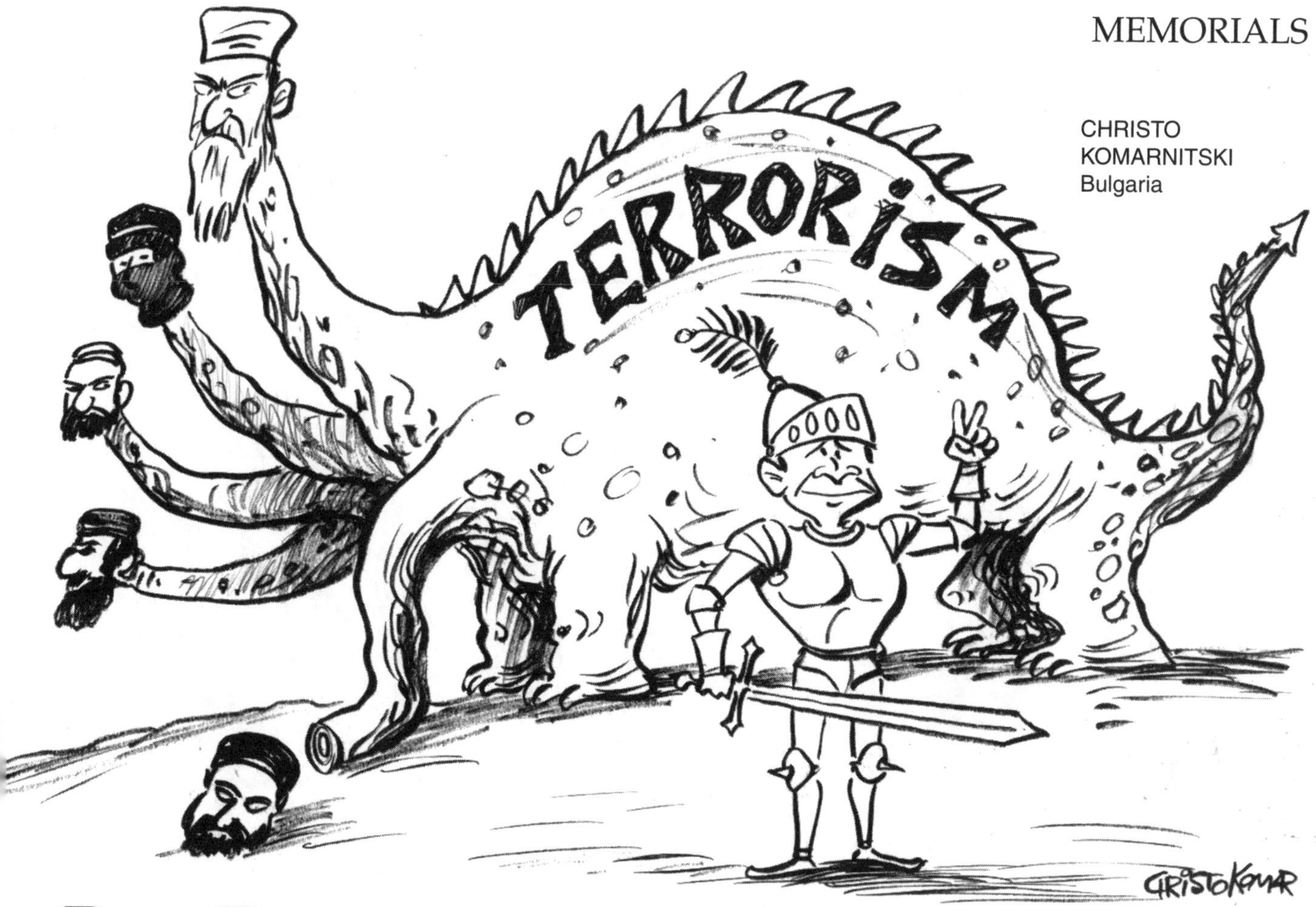
TERRORISM
CHRISTOKOMAR

YAAKOV KIRSCHEN
Jerusalem Post

Dry Bones
TROUBLE IN PARADISE
!$%#!?!
?
IT'S ZARQAWI! WE GAVE HIM HIS SEVENTY WHITE RAISINS...
BUT HE KEEPS DEMANDING "VIRGINS"!
IT'S THAT DAMNED MIS-TRANSLATION AGAIN!
!$%#!?!

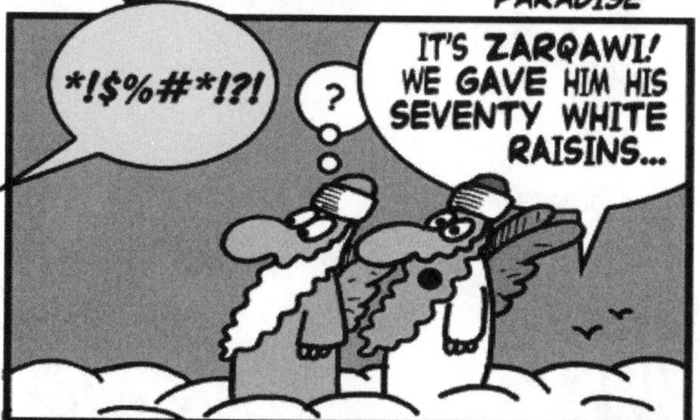

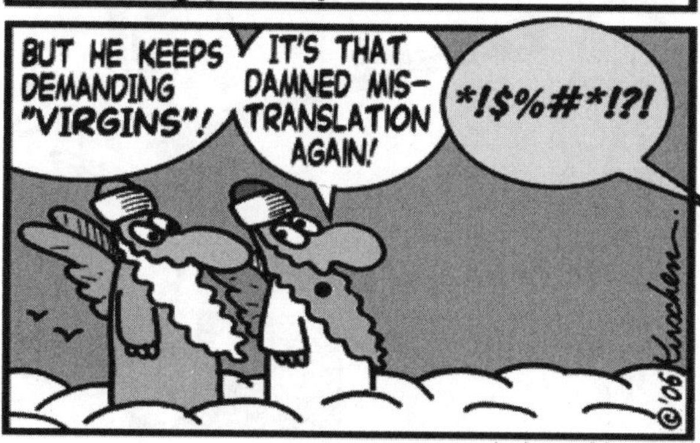

HENRY PAYNE
Detroit News

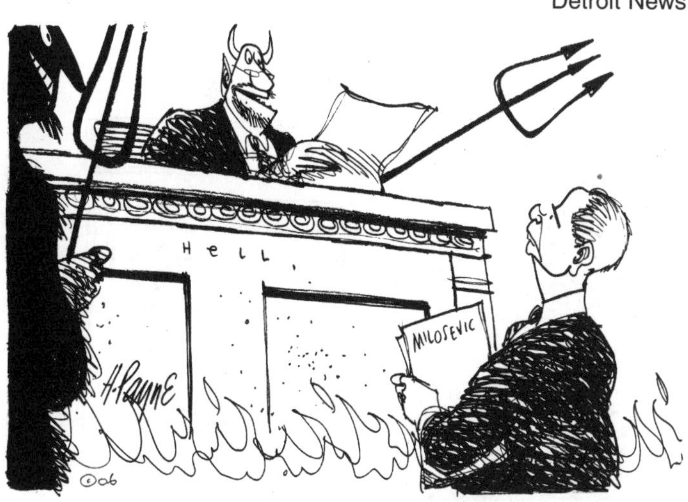

HELL
MILOSEVIC
H. PAYNE
©06
"IT SEEMS YOU DIED BEFORE YOUR WAR-CRIMES TRIAL WAS COMPLETE. FORTUNATELY, I HAVE YOUR SENTENCE RIGHT HERE..."

FREDERICK DELIGNE
Nice-Matin, France

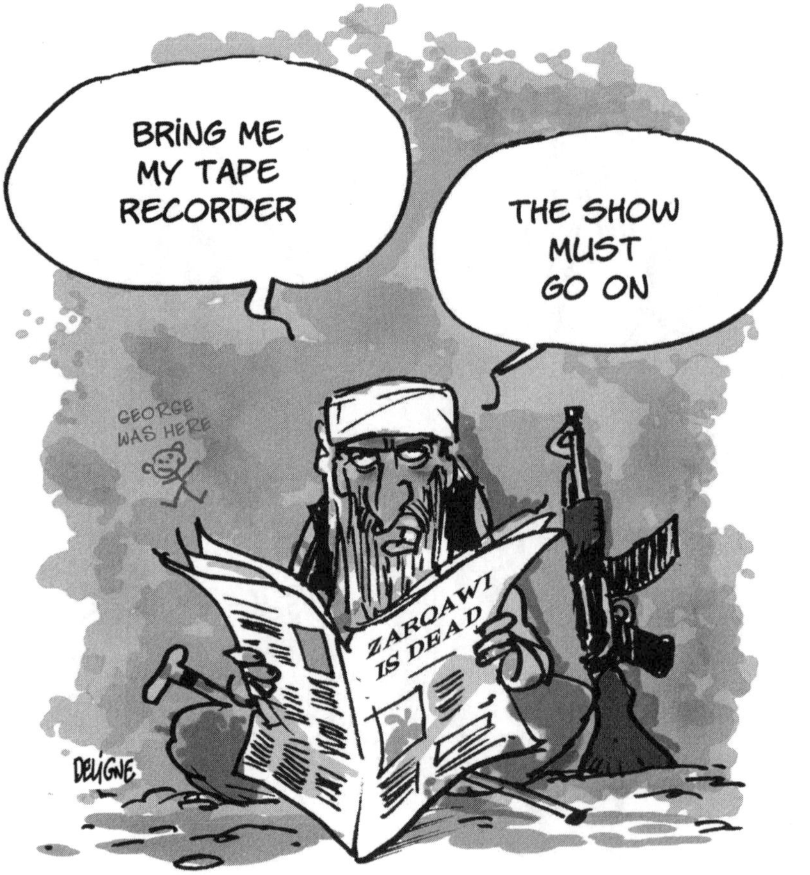
BRING ME MY TAPE RECORDER
THE SHOW MUST GO ON
GEORGE WAS HERE
ZARQAWI IS DEAD
DELIGNE

ROBERT ARIAIL
The State (SC)

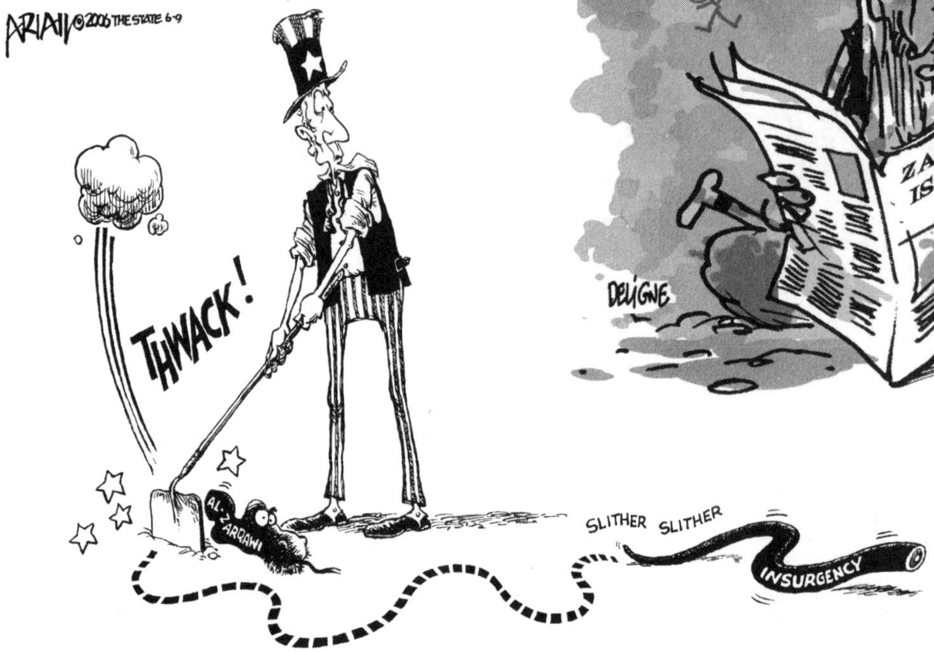
ARIAIL ©2006 THE STATE 6-9
THWACK!
AL-ZARQAWI
SLITHER SLITHER
INSURGENCY

ADAM ZYGLIS, Buffalo News

THEN...
NOW...
THIS IMAGE IS TOO OFFENSIVE!
PRESS
ZARQAWI
SNAP
SNAP
SNAP
POP
ADAM ZYGLIS ©2006 THE BUFFALO NEWS
www.adamzyglis.com

BRIAN ADCOCK, Scotland

AL-QAIDA IN IRAQ LOSES IT'S HEAD....

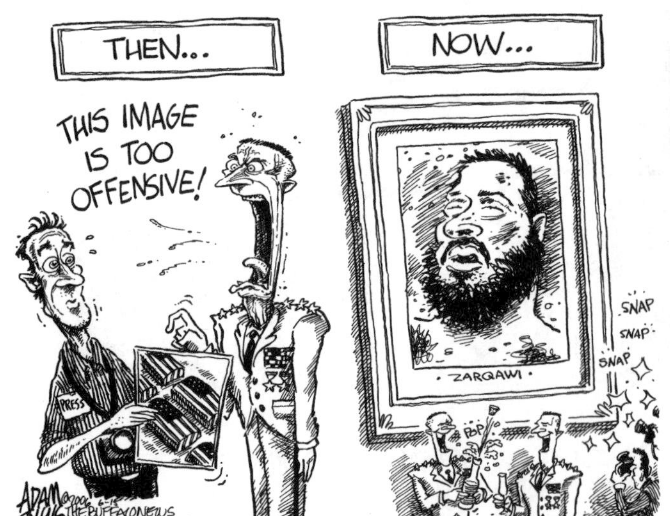

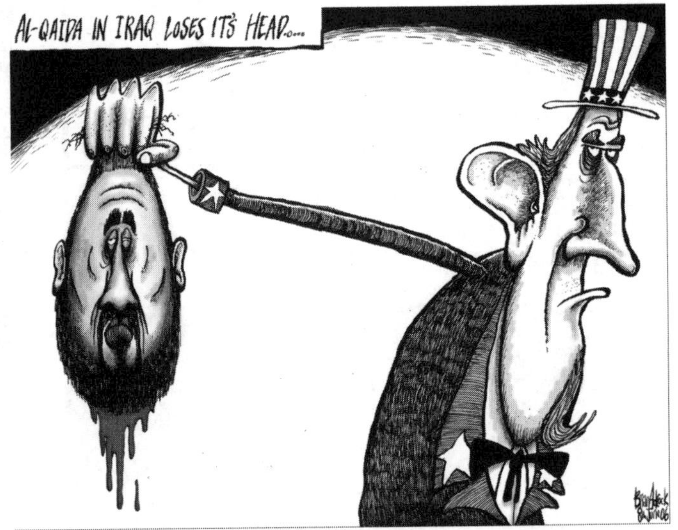

HENRY PAYNE, Detroit News

ROB ROGERS
Pittsburgh Post-Gazette

CHAN LOWE, South Florida Sun-Sentinel

JEFF STAHLER
Columbus Dispatch

DANA SUMMERS, Orlando Sentinel

Artists Index

You can see a complete archive of each cartoonist's work on our web site at www.cagle.com. Come take a look! Want to contact a cartoonist or ask for premission to reproduce a cartoon? Contact information for each cartoonist accompanies their cartoons on www.cagle.com.